Early Praise for *Great White Elephant*™

"Franco has done it again! If you ever had that nagging feeling inside that you were actually doing harm to your children every time you said 'yes' to them, then this book is for you. Franco does a brilliant job of helping you discover the 'Great White Elephants' in your life and reframing the negative and destructive beliefs and behaviors that can come from ownership, power, and money. Within these chapters you will learn to install a process into your life that will enhance your legacy with your family for generations."

MICHAEL VICKERS, Speaker, educator, father, and best-selling author of
Becoming Preferred: How to Outsell Your Competition, Phoenix, AZ

"In his most recent book, *Great White Elephant*,™ Mr. Lombardo identifies road blocks to successful wealth transition. In a very interesting analysis of the estate planning process, he establishes new and powerful techniques for overcoming the suppressed and unspoken issues which can create chasms between parent and child."

WILLIAM M. BONE, President
Canadian Business Family Office

"*Great White Elephant*™ will stimulate your thinking about parenting children of wealth and provide practical ideas to help you manage the challenges of wealth."

ANDREW D. KEYT, Executive Director,
Family Business Center, Loyola University, Chicago, IL

"*Great White Elephant!™ Why Rich Kids Hate Their Parents* is a provocative title fit for a book that challenges parents, their successors, and their advisors to think differently about succession and wealth transition. Regardless of the size of your fortune, Lombardo's message is one that deserves your attention: wealth transition is not something you just check off your list. It's a lifelong journey requiring introspection, hard work, and a commitment to building relationships. This book is a thoughtful, caring, and abundantly clear road map on how to accomplish these goals."

MIKE McGRANN, Executive Director,
S. Dale High Center for Family Business, Elizabethtown, PA

"Parenting is challenging enough in today's high-tech, low conversation environment. When you add significant wealth that will be transferred to future generations and avoidance of the wealth owners "white elephants," you create a deadly cocktail that not only destroys the wealth that may have taken generations to create, but the emotional health of the family as well. By examining this subject, Franco shares numerous client stories and examples that can offer a framework that will better prepare these family members for transition. In addition, he explores a subject most advisors are neither trained to nor willing to address. This is an important book and a must-read for both families and their advisors."

BRIAN J. D. HUGHES, President & Founder,
Hughes Growth Strategies, LLC, Philadelphia, PA

"Wow! At last a step-by-step book for success with your kids. *Great White Elephant™* is Franco's third book. Read this book! Learn, gain wisdom, and develop better understanding with your children. I did!"

DR. PETER LEGGE, OBC, LLD (Hon), D. Tech,
Businessman, speaker, and author, Vancouver, BC

"*Great White Elephant* encourages readers to explore and understand the motivations behind their own behaviors—an important first step towards productive, fulfilling relationships with others. The author, by being brutally honest about his own life-long journey of self-discovery, provides an example for others.

"The statistics are well documented—less than 10% of family-owned businesses are successful at transitioning their wealth to the third generation. What is not as well understood and documented is that the vast majority of the reasons for these failures lie within the family itself. These are the 'Great White Elephants' that families avoid discussing and Franco Lombardo has tackled head-on in this ground-breaking book. Those who read it and apply the principles presented will be well equipped to dramatically improve the odds of success in their favor."

"Are my values aligned with my valuables?" Franco Lombardo is spot on! He brings the challenge of succession planning, family dynamics, and how wealth plays such a powerful role in our relationships with those that really matter in our lives...our children."

"This is a wonderful read. The informal style draws you in, and the content is clearly presented and allows the reader to work along with the presentation, making the book even more rewarding. This is not just a book for the wealthy but for every family who is raising kids through adulthood, on how to create thoughtful, sensitive, and responsible kids."

DENNIS JAFFE, PhD, Professor of Organizational Systems and Psychology, Saybrook University, San Francisco, CA

"This book is a must-read for anyone with wealth and a family. The only regret is that Franco didn't write this book 10 years ago."

JOHN H. ASKIN, Wealth Strategy Planner, *Wealth Strategy Group*, Vancouver, BC

"*Great White Elephant*™ is full of thought-provoking questions and stimulating real-life stories that would benefit any business family embarking on the succession journey or simply wanting to improve their family relationships."

DON ZINYK, FCA, Executive Professor, *Alberta Business Family Institute*, University of Alberta, Edmonton, AB

FRANCO LOMBARDO

Author of *Money Motto:*™ *The Path to Authentic Wealth*™*!*
& Life after Wealth:® *When is Enough Enough?*

Great White Elephant™

Why Rich Kids Hate Their Parents!

with a Foreword by

ROY O. WILLIAMS, THE WILLIAMS GROUP

Co-author of *Philanthropy, Heirs & Values* and *Preparing Heirs*

ROPER HOUSE PUBLISHING
Vancouver, British Columbia

Published by Roper House Publishing
To contact the publisher, please visit:
www.moneymotto.com
or e-mail: francol@veritage.ca

Life after Wealth,® Money Motto,™ Authentic Wealth™ and Great White Elephant™ are registered trademarks of Roper House Publishing.

Library and Archives Canada Cataloguing in Publication

Lombardo, Franco 1965–
    Great white elephant: why rich kids hate their parents / Franco Lombardo, with a foreword by Roy O. Williams.

Includes bibliographical references.
ISBN 978–0–9731061–0–7

 A CIP record has been applied for and is available from the publisher by request.

TECHNICAL CREDITS:
WRITING ASSISTANCE: Jeremy Drought, *Last Impression Publishing Service*, Calgary, Alberta
COVER, INTERIOR DESIGN & PRODUCTION: Jeremy Drought, Last Impression Publishing Service, Calgary, Alberta
COPYEDITING & PROOFREADING: Sandy Gough, *Sanscript Communication Studio Inc.* Calgary, Alberta
Printed and bound in Canada by *Friesens Corporation*, Altona, Manitoba

* * *

This book is presented to:

_____

by:

_____

* * *

DEDICATION

Courage is the power to let go of the familiar.

RAYMOND LINDQUIST

IF WE ARE BRAVE ENOUGH TO LEAVE THE COMFORTABLE and familiar behind—and this could mean leaving our thoughts and ideas, our relationships, and all of our material possessions behind—and risk the misunderstanding, lack of forgiveness and resentment of others, while we embark on a truth-seeking journey (both internally and externally) with a willingness to accept that everything that happens does so for a reason, and where everyone we meet has something to teach us, and we are prepared to face up to and then forgive ourselves for all our faults and shortcomings, then the truth shall not be withheld from us.

I know this to be true, for I have ventured on such a journey. Writing this book has transformed my life in such a way that, at times, I no longer always easily recognize myself. I have experienced the peaks of victory as well as the valleys of defeat. In the process, along the way, I have found my truth. My intention is that you may find your own truth and set yourself free from the Great White Elephants in your life.

I'd like to share this story with you:

The Great Spirit gathered all of the creatures together. There was a question the Great Spirit wanted to present to his brothers and sisters. "I have a request. There is something I want to place in a special place for its owner to one day find. This something is of great value to its owner, and yet it is illusive to most. I am looking for suggestions as to where to place this gift."

The bear stood up and said: "I will hold it in my jowls and with it climb to the highest of peaks, and hide it there."

"That is a great idea brother," replied Great Spirit, "but one day the owner will climb to the highest peaks and find it there."

A salmon spoke from the water and suggested: "I will carry it between my fins and swim to the depths of the ocean, and place it there."

"My sister," Great Spirit replied, "Good idea, but one day the owner will dive to the depths of the ocean and find it there."

The eagle, speaking from the top of a tree, suggested: "I will place it in my talons and fly it to the moon, and hide it there."

"My cousin," Great Spirit replied, "that is a fine idea, but one day, man will build an eagle and fly to the moon and find this treasure there."

Finally, a mole poked its head from its hole and said:

"I know, put it in him, that way only the most brave and courageous will have the vulnerability to find their own truth, within themselves."

I share this story with you, because this book is dedicated to you the reader and fellow traveler. We are all on a journey, the journey to find ourselves, our own truth and ultimately love ourselves again.

This book is dedicated to those who have the courage to go in search of their own truth. Yes, I am talking about *you*! Something in you drew you to these pages and this journey with me. Know that it is both my privilege and an honor to be your Sherpa as you explore with me.

ACKNOWLEDGEMENTS

MY DEEP, SINCERE, AND HUMBLE ACKNOWLEDGMENTS to the following people, programs, organizations, and events in my life that have supported and sustained me during the writing of this book:

To my children, Gabby and Mateo—by far the greatest gift in my life—who have seen me laugh and cry, be happy and sad, experience joy and regret, and just stood resolute beside me and hugged their dad during a very dark time in my life.

To Trudy who taught me the capacity I have to love another, so fully and passionately. It is thanks to Trudy that I have discovered my truth of being safe and valuable on my own two feet.

To my parents, Lila Reyes and Angelo Lombardo, who did a fantastic job in raising me. It is thanks to them meeting on a blind date, falling in love, and creating me that you have these pages in front of you. It is also because of what they were unable to provide, that I am the man, the father, and partner I am today. I finally learned how to feel all of my feelings.

To *Landmark Education* and their Introduction Leaders Program, where I really learned: "without integrity, nothing works." Painful and personally costly as this lesson was, I get it now.

To my coach and mentor, Dov Baron, whose compassionate straightforwardness has helped shape me to be the man, father, and coach I am today. Dov is the father I never had and so desperately needed and longed for.

To Ren, Dov's wife, queen and partner, whose strength has given me strength when I did not have it or could not find it in myself. Her tender voice kept me here when I was ready to check out.

To my dear friend Al, my brother from another mother, who one day took me for coffee and said to me: "Franco, I see you as operating at only 2% of your capacity." Thank you for shepherding me towards accessing much more of my other 98%. It is thanks to you and your love for me, that this book is here.

To brother Frank, WOW! Thank you for being the light in my life on those very dark, scary, and lonely days. Your compassion and true grit pulled me through, when I felt I could not go on.

To dear and close friends, Terry and Santina, for opening your home to me, so that I may express my feelings in a safe, and compassionate place.

To Bill and Fran, who are my home away from home. Bill, thank you for your listening to me when I shared my secrets and desires in my weakest moments. I felt safe, listened to, and I knew I could count on you both.

To my friend and business partner, Richard, thank you for believing in me and in all that we do at Veritage. It is in our work here we have the capacity to facilitate great change in the lives of our clients.

To Lorraine (LC), my right hand, and trusted confidant, thank you for listening to me, and for your gracious, loving but tough advice. You have taught me not to be the needy girlfriend!

To BN and FN, thank you for being my "brothers" in strength and in humor.

To all of my client-families in my private practice, thank you for trusting me sufficiently as to allow me into your lives in such a vulnerable way. It is you who inspire me to continue to do what I love to do. Thank you for the privilege and honor of being of service to you.

To Jeremy, my publishing consultant and book designer, my avatar and sage, who compassionately challenged my theories, thoughts, and writing. He has been the backbone of this project, being a calming and supportive influence as I journeyed along with my thoughts and feelings, dealing with my Great White Elephants, and encouraging me to keep clarifying and refining my ideas.

To *The Executive Committee (TEC)*, the *Young Presidents' Organization (YPO)*, and *The Canadian Institute of Chartered Accountants (CICA)*, as well as *The Society Of Estate and Trust Practitioners (STEP)*, for each providing me with the opportunity to speak to your members. Thank you for inviting me.

To you, the reader, thank you for trusting yourself and giving yourself permission to be drawn to this book. Thank you for your inquisitiveness and courage to seek out and face your own Great White Elephants.

To all those who so generously provided a testimonial or endorsement of this book, thank you for believing in my message.

Finally, I salute myself, for having the courage and strength to face my own vulnerability and deal with my greatest white elephant—that of never feeling safe or valuable. In having the desire to influence and, hopefully, positively change my own world as a result of writing this book, I trust it will also have a positive influence upon lives of others. Through this very personal journey I have learned to love myself and am proud to declare it.

Franco Lombardo
White Rock, BC
March 2012

CONTENTS

• Dedication ix

• Acknowledgements.. xiii

• Foreword by Roy O. Williams xix

• Preface... xxi

♦ ♦ ♦

• Introduction 1

1 My Great White Elephant:™
   The Ownership Myth 15

2 Values and Valuables 49

3 A Tale of Perspectives 87

4 The Money Motto 109

5 Finding Our Power in the Missing Conversation......... 135

• Conclusion 167

♦ ♦ ♦

• Suggested Readings 171

• About the Book.. 175

• About the Author.. 177

• For More Information 181

• About *Life after Wealth:® When is Enough Enough?* 183

• About *Money Motto:™ The Path to Authentic Wealth™!* 187

FOREWORD

by Roy O. Williams, The Williams Group

FRANCO HAS WRITTEN AN INSPIRING, SELF-REFLECTING BOOK on the communication breakdowns in families and the transfer of wealth. Franco's compassionate stories are intertwined with the psychology of his experience and those of his clients.

The stories and related experiences are well articulated and designed to motivate and make family leaders aware of the blind spots they may have. The white elephant is a great idiom most will recognize and relate to.

My perspective is that *Great White Elephant*™ will become a wonderful tool for making family leaders aware of the gaping and grasping hole in most estate plans, worldwide.

Roy O. Williams
Founder of The Williams Group
Stockton & San Clemente, California
April 2012

PREFACE

Before you get started, I want to clarify that not all rich kids hate their parents! A lot of them do though. As a parent, you might ask, why is this the case? If I have worked hard to provide my family with all of the comforts of life and supported a grand lifestyle, then what have I done to be hated by my kids? The answer lies not in what you have done or given, but in what you have not done or given. When children are asked what they want most from a parent, it's not material possessions or more "toys," or even cold, hard cash; it's through the time you spend together that they know they are loved.

Another reason that could contribute to rich kids hating their parents is the lack of boundary setting that many parents fail to implement for their children while they are growing up. Basically, what I mean by boundary setting is the ability to say "no" to a child's request for something. Boundaries of all sorts are usually established to help keep us safe. At any point in time, they come to represent the line that must not be crossed which determines what we can and cannot do, what we can and can't expect. Having two children of my own, I know how hard it can be to say no to a request from one of my children, especially if I can afford to grant the request—temporally, materially, or financially. However, during the twenty odd years over which we raise our children if we do not say "no" enough, we may end up finding out that we fostered some rather unfortunate expectations in our offspring and did them a great disservice in the long run. To have raised children who come to learn (and expect) that every request they ever make will be granted with bells on, is a recipe for significant resentment when they find out that the rest of the world might not be so generous in accommodating their every whim and fancy.

Rationally, most all of us know that they cannot expect the rest of the world to indulge them all of the time, and nor should we, as their parents, regardless of whether we can afford to do so. If you can afford to do so, more's the reason you probably shouldn't over-indulge your children.

It is in saying "no" and establishing some boundaries that we instill some better sense of having measured expectations that prepare our children for life. Sometimes, we have to show our children we love them by saying "no" as opposed to "yes" all the time. This teaches them that they will not always get what they want when they want it. As I have worked with some of the world's wealthiest families I have seen first hand the impact of the "yes" parents as opposed to the "no" parents.

I'm not saying that a simple "yes" and a simple "no" are actually always the best and only answers to provide. Actually, it is in witnessing your struggle to come up with an answer to a request—some deliberation and reflection—that children actually come to learn they are valued and loved. If they see you taking a bit of time to respond to their requests, and the answer is a qualified "yes" or "no," with some limits or provisos, like you met them part way, then they will also have learned two other important things: a) that their request was heard and b) you care about them enough to struggle with the process of coming up with an appropriate response. Furthermore, it is through the responses you give to their requests that they will, in time, learn about your values and end up having some themselves. This is a great way to reduce the number of Great White Elephants that will move in if you only and always answer with a "yes" or a "no!"

When I am referring to the "yes" parents, I am referring to those who for whatever reasons, always had a difficult time saying "no" to any of their children's requests. Typically the children of these parents will grow up with resentments or feelings of anger towards their parents, and will have a much higher, overbearing sense of their own entitlement.

The parents who managed to say "no" some of the time; those of you who have denied some of your children's requests, or made the granting of them conditional—they had to work for or earn some of their privileges and gifts, will typically have more well adjusted children who will have learned to value and respect what money and wealth can do. Such children will tend to have a more moderate sense of their own entitlement. They will also have a tendency to express more gratitude towards their parents and life in general.

This book is written with one goal in mind, to assist you in increasing your odds of success with respect to passing on your wealth or the ownership of your business to the next generation—your own children. If you are an inheritor, or prospective inheritor, then this book is also written for you to increase the odds of you feeling worthy and safe and your being prepared to receive wealth or assume ownership of the family business.

Contrary to popular, current industry practices, I firmly believe there is a much better way—and perhaps it's the only way—to successfully bequeath wealth to your children. The hallmarks of this better way require of those involved the ability to implement the process of wealth transition consciously, intentionally, and with a deep sense of love and in a state of generosity. Being mindful of the power of these emotional conditions also serves to create a more appropriate climate for wealth transition since they facilitate receptivity in those to whom the gift of wealth is to be bequeathed, and enable them to grasp the spirit of intention with a similar sense of love and in a similar state of generosity.

With this in mind, I ask you to consider the following fundamental question: What is love? Clearly there are myriad definitions and descriptions of what love might be, and there is no single, right answer. Here are a few sources and ideas to get you started.

In the first book of Corinthians, Chapter 13, Verses 4–7, the Holy Bible states:

> "Love is patient. Love is kind. It does not envy, it does not boast, it is not proud. It does not dishonor others, it is not self-seeking, it is not easily angered, it keeps no records of wrong. Love does not delight in evil, but rejoices in truth. It always protects, always trusts, always hopes, always preserves."

Webster's Dictionary defines love as: "A strong affection for another arising out of kinship or personal ties."

More precisely, the question you might wish to ponder as you navigate the pages of this book is a bit more personal: What is love to you? How is it, exactly, that you show or demonstrate to those you think and/or say you love—that you indeed love them, including yourself?

From the perspective of those you say you love, do you know what love is or means to them? In his book *The Five Love Languages*, author Gary Chapman explains and describes in great detail the five ways he feels we all show and receive love.

These five main languages of love, as described by Gary Chapman, are as follows:

- *Time.* An individual feels love when time is spent with them.

- *Acts of Service.* One feels loved when acts of service are done for them.
- *Words of Affirmation.* One is told they are loved or affirmed verbally.
- *Gifts.* One is bought gifts to show love.
- *Physical Touch.* One feels love when they are physically touched, and this does not have to be in a sexual context.

Gary explains how each one of us has a primary love language, that is the way we feel loved. Typically one's love language is also how one shows and expresses their love to another.

Given these variables in the way we each show and receive love, it would seem to make complete sense to first clarify how each of your children—or those to whom you intend to bequeath your wealth and/or the family business—individually show and receive love. You need to understand their language of love before ever you start to consider the more mechanical, technical aspects of wealth transition.

What is generosity to you? *Webster's Dictionary* defines generosity as: "The habit of giving. Often equated with charity as a virtue, generosity is widely accepted in society as a desirable habit. Generosity can also be spending time, money, or labor, for others, without being rewarded in return."

There has to be a better way to transition wealth, one which is more effective and efficient than the current model. I say this with some conviction in light of current industry statistics that state more than 70% of business successions fail from the first to the second generation. This is not because these families have necessarily received poor professional advice. In point of fact, more often than not, such families have typically received professional advice from some of the best advisors in the industry—an observation that only begs us to dig deeper still to find a reason for that dismal rate of failure.

Generally speaking, when it comes to advice on wealth transition and business succession planning, the current focus within the succession planning industry is nearly always upon the technical aspects of the process. This approach is driven by the structural and tax-related issues, and typically never takes into account the emotions of the individuals involved. The analogy that I use when either I speak to a group or am in the midst of a private consultation with a client is this: the tactical, technical wealth transition plan is merely a tabletop discussion. It's a conversation about the facts, figures, forms, ledgers, and laws that literally cover the top of the table. I call this "top of the table planning." It's a conversation that pays no heed to the underlying emotional issues of the people for and with whom that tabletop discussion is being held, or for whom any wealth transition or business succession plan is being designed. Most of the time, the emotional affect of those involved is not even considered, never mind appropriately addressed.

My analogy suggests that it is the unexamined feelings and emotions of those involved which can ultimately topple the table and animate the Great White Elephants. Your values—identifying and clarifying what they are—are the metaphorical legs supporting the tabletop. Without strong, solidly defined values you have weak legs underneath that tabletop (discussion) and any top of the table plan you make will likely collapse; maybe not immediately, but it's only a matter of time before it will, and it does so more than 70% of the time. In a direct sense, then, unchecked Great White Elephants topple tables. So, you've got to take care of your *values* as well as your *valuables* to be successful with your business succession planning and the transfer of wealth to the next generation.

I wrote this book because I have witnessed the fallout costs of too many grand plans that have ultimately failed and far too many broken families—wherein rich kids *do* hate their parents! This has caused me great sadness and I have made it my mission and professional contribution to assist with the healing of families, as there is no greater bond than that of family. I did not get to experience this with my family, so it is my desire that you will experience it with your family and create love and connection between each other.

In their book, *For Love and/or Money: The Impact of Inherited Wealth on Relationships*, Barbara Blouin and Katherine Gibson write at great length about the struggles faced by those who have or are destined to inherit wealth and they provide numerous examples of how the current approach to preparing for wealth transition is not working. There is plenty of supporting evidence for such a bold statement. The results of a study entitled *First Success Readiness Survey of Canadian Family-owned Businesses* by the Deloitte Centre for Tax Education and Research at the School of Accounting and Finance, University of Waterloo (1999) and another, *The BDO Dunwoody/COMPAS Report on Canadian Family-owned Business* (2003) each clearly paint a picture of poor success rates in wealth transition.

My intention for you, if you are of the older, founding generation, is to have you connect with the reason/s why you built and accumulated your wealth in the first place, and connect this with what you really want and desire for your children or successors. As the parent/s and benefactor/s, what is it that you can do to intellectually and emotionally prepare the next generation so that they may be ready to receive the wealth which you have spent a lifetime accumulating?

If you are someone who stands to be a beneficiary of inherited wealth, my intention for you is to have you recognize more fully than you already may, the gift your parents represent, and for you to be ready and prepared to receive the gift of wealth with sincere love and gratitude, and in state of complete ease, without any guilt, remorse, or ill feelings, so that you might see the gift for what it is—a gift.

In his inaugural speech, Nelson Mandela quoted Marianne Williamson:

"Our deepest fear is not that we are inadequate. Our deepest fear is that we are powerful beyond measure. It is our light, not our darkness that most frightens us. We ask ourselves: who am I to be brilliant, gorgeous, talented, or fabulous? Actually who are we not to be? You are a child of God. Your playing small does not serve the world. There is nothing enlightening about shrinking so that others wouldn't feel insecure around you. We are all meant to shine as children do. We are born to manifest the glory of God that is within us. It's not just in some of us. It's in everyone. And as we let our light shine, we unconsciously give others permission to do the same. And as we are liberated from our fears, our presence automatically liberates others."

My suggestion to all you benefactors is that your wealth can be used to empower your children to find, claim, and embrace their greatness.

Great White Elephant™ will show you how to better manage the transition of your wealth to your children or grandchildren, and achieve that with enduring love and abundant generosity. This book will also show you how you might best ensure that what really matters to you has been fully expressed, that your intentions have been clearly articulated and understood, and ultimately, that your actions are fully aligned with your fundamental values.

My desire is that you will be become curiously engaged and wholly playful through your wealth transition process. Remember the "why." Be intentional about the process; imbue it with love and a sense of generosity; do all this and stand back and witness what good you can set in motion. Nothing trumps love!

Franco Lombardo
White Rock, BC
March 2012

INTRODUCTION

"When the world says give up, hope whispers try one more time."

— Unknown —

The Elephant in the Room

"It's not who you think you are that holds you back,
it's who you think you are not."

— Unknown —

WIKIPEDIA INTERPRETS THE "ELEPHANT IN THE ROOM" as an English metaphorical idiom for an obvious truth that is either being ignored or remains unaddressed. The idiomatic expression also appears to suggest an obvious problem or issue that no one wants to discuss. It is based on the idea that an elephant in a room would be impossible to overlook, and thus people in the room have to pretend it is not there and have clearly chosen to avoid dealing with the present and pressing issue.

A "white elephant" is an idiom for a valuable but burdensome possession that the owner cannot easily dispose of and whose cost (particularly the cost of upkeep) is out of all proportion to its utility. White elephants (albino elephants) have long been regarded as sacred in Thailand and throughout Southeast Asia. The upkeep and maintenance of a white elephant was an expensive undertaking, since the owner had to provide for its special dietary needs as well as provide access to people who wanted to come and worship the revered beast. If a Thai king became dissatisfied with a subject, he would sometimes give him a white elephant. Such a gift as this, in most cases, would lead to the financial (economic) ruin of the recipient. Since the white elephant was regarded as sacred and frequently worshiped by the masses, as a gift, it really was considered both blessing and curse.

I chose to make use of the idiom of a white elephant in this book since it neatly represents the problematic issues that most families typically choose to ignore, and seek to avoid discussing or addressing as they confront the process of family business succession planning and successful wealth transition.

When I begin working with a family (for succession planning and wealth transition purposes) typically, I intentionally guide the conversation towards the identification of the "Great White Elephants"—all of the troublesome, unspoken, and particularly problematic issues (the skeletons in the closet) for the family, and I usually receive the following reactions: fear, disbelief, and then excitement, as the family members realize they are actually going to deal with whatever it is that has been hanging over them like a dark cloud for as long as anyone can remember, which can be, in some cases, a matter of decades.

I would like you to consider that the Great White Elephant™ most commonly uncovered in wealthy families is usually representative of things like the responsibility of ownership, money, and power. As the myth goes, if one is given a white elephant, which could be seen as too much power, money, or responsibility, the gift rapidly becomes a burden that could ultimately destroy the recipient.

This book is an opportunity for me to share some classic examples of the myriad ways in which families, with whom I have had the privilege of working, have faced up to and managed their own Great White Elephants. The need to face up to the truth is not always easy or plain sailing, but I will show you a process for dealing with and ultimately embracing your own Great White Elephant™ so that you can be free of its burden and potentially tyrannical influence on you and your family.

Great White Elephant:™ *Why Rich Kids Hate their Parents* is really about owning up to the fact that you have a Great White Elephant™ of your own. Once you have identified your Great White Elephant,™ and got clear about what its needs are, and what must be in place to release it, you've begun the process of laying down a foundation for succession planning and the eventual successful transition of wealth. As a benefactor, knowing what you have to bequeath and all that it entails, is only part of the process. For succession planning and wealth transition to be successful, you also have to ensure your beneficiaries—the next generation—are appropriately equipped and fully committed to the release and resolution of the Great White Elephant.™

It is also of the utmost importance then, that all members of the family—both the older generation and the younger generation—get clear on how each of them actually sees (defines) the Great White Elephant.™ Every member of the family will have their own unique perspective or point of view on the Great White Elephant,™ whether it is a matter of business ownership, power, or money, or some combination of all three.

The next step is for every stakeholder to identify how they presently behave around the Great White Elephant™— particularly if any aspect of their behavior places a negative impact on the business and the family.

The Way It Is

> *Courage is what it takes to stand up and speak;*
> *courage is also what it takes to sit down and listen.*
> — WINSTON CHURCHILL —

This book is about finding courage, making connections, and navigating transitions. It is about you finding the courage to acknowledge the Great White Elephant™ in your family; and your willingness to deal effectively with the Great White Elephant™

so that it does not destroy your family. It is about making new connections, including the relationship you have with yourself, your business, your wealth, and the relationships you have with the members of the next generation—the ones who will be inheriting the wealth you spent a lifetime creating. It is also about the process you will be going through or perhaps have already gone through in navigating the succession planning process and the transition of your wealth.

Most importantly, this book is about first having the courage to say: Yes, I acknowledge that we—as a family—have this Great White Elephant,™ and then making a commitment to engage in a conversation to embrace it as opposed to ignoring it, and pretending it is not in the room…because it is!

Furthermore, those professional advisors who serve wealthy families need to access their own courage if they are to help a family acknowledge and address their familial Great White Elephant.™ Most professionals who in some manner work with their clients with respect to addressing issues of succession planning and/or the transition of wealth, will start out by dealing with all of the technical aspects of the succession plan such as the tax implications, the structural efficiency of the plan required to bequeath ownership of the assets to maximum advantage etc., whether it be a family business under discussion, or a large portfolio of investments. Many professionals achieve success at doing all of this and do it all with a high degree of competency. But that is all they do! It follows, logically so, that this sort of succession planning advice is about the sum total of what most clients have heard and received from advisors and naturally, they too assume that this is the way things are done and are the only issues that need to be addressed. In terms of professional practice, therefore, the way things have always been done, and the way things largely continue to be done means most clients also continue to assume that this is the right and only way.

And yet, here I sit, wanting to challenge the tradition and conventional ways of dealing with succession planning and the transfer of wealth. Based on the results of some key industry research projects and my own experience, I feel that the traditional methodologies for dealing with succession planning and the transfer of wealth are simply not working. You need only look at some of the statistics to recognize this fact.

By starting out with a "top of the table" discussion, both families and advisors get caught up with all of these technical issues and quickly become trapped. As a consequence, they end up planning for succession and the transition of wealth to the next generation, often with exceedingly complex structures, all to try and ensure that the maximum proportion of current wealth is transferred as smoothly and as equitably as possible, especially whenever there are multiple recipients or beneficiaries in the succeeding generation.

What I have witnessed as lacking is a deep, often profoundly moving discussion about an alternative sort of process that actually underpins (or should underpin) any "top of the table" planning. This alternative process is about dealing with the human, emotional side of succession planning and the transfer of wealth. How does any parent know that their children (who could be in their forties or fifties at the time of transfer) are prepared to inherit wealth? What have these parents done to prepare the next generation, both intellectually and emotionally, to successfully inherit anything?

A survey conducted by my firm to investigate people's feelings about money led us to discover that one of the greatest fears harbored by wealthy parents is whether or not they have done a proper job of preparing their children to inherit wealth? Here's the catch. Almost universally, parents cannot clearly articulate what having prepared their children means or looks like in practical terms. The analogy I use to illustrate this conundrum is the following: imagine you have just purchased a brand new Ferrari for your sixteen-year-old. Your child has seen this car on TV and in the movies, and perhaps read about it in automotive magazines. You decided that adequate preparation for buying the car would involve introducing your child to the designer, to members of the assembly team, and the CEO of Ferrari, all so your child could develop some understanding and background education about this advanced piece of high performance transportation.

Once this technical education is complete, you know your child could easily regurgitate any detail concerning the technical specifications of the vehicle, tell you both the rationale for the design as well as how it was assembled and quite possibly also share with you the future plans of the Ferrari company. You know he/she knows all this, because you arranged for the best technical advisors available to educate him/her.

So, with this technical education complete and newfound knowledge at their fingertips, you, the parent, feel confident that you can toss your beloved offspring the keys and tell them to take it for a spin! Perhaps your child already has some experience in driving a car. Before their solo outing in the Ferrari, you did some laps with them in the family Audi, practiced parallel parking in an empty lot of the neighborhood mall, and ensured they had taken Driver's Education in high school; all good preparation for the driving test that will qualify him/her for an operator's license.

Yet, here he is, sitting in a sophisticated, powerful performance vehicle, getting ready to take it out and experience for the first time, all of the power that this car has the capacity to deliver. Would you let him go and drive it based on what he has learned from the technical advisors at Ferrari? Of course not! At least not in your right mind! What he is missing is the experience of driving a car like this; experiencing the power of acceleration, the pull on one's body as you move through a corner, the precise shifting of the gears and so on. I'm sure you get the picture.

And yet this is just how most parents prepare their children to inherit wealth or take over the running of the family enterprise. I propose there is a better way—the right way. That right way is one in which the "top of the table" issues are fully addressed and everything is dealt with in the most structurally efficient, advantageous and equitable fashion, but that all of this is done *after* the legs of the table are firmly in place, which means the *values* are identified and clarified and the emotional challenges—including the confrontation of the Great White Elephants—are dealt with so those legs are both strong and sturdy. Those legs should also be sufficiently flexible as to accommodate the changing needs of the family and the ever-volatile economic environment, both of which inevitably dictate that the "top of the table" elements are continuously reviewed. To clarify then, your Great White Elephants are all of the emotional issues that families tend to avoid—the awkward conversations, the unspoken feelings that, if addressed, would clear the air. It is when these sorts of issues (skeletons in the closet or elephants in the room) remain unaddressed that they tend to undermine the "top of the table" planning—everything slides off when the legs are not strong and steady! Family values, once clearly identified and agreed upon, are the legs of the table that ensure it can support the "top of the table" planning that is eventually guided by the professionals.

The Way It Could Be

> *Nothing in life is to be feared. It is only to be understood.*
> — MARIE CURIE —

What if the whole process of succession planning and wealth transition began with a discussion designed to help a client identify the Great White Elephant™ in their own nuclear family? What if such a discussion supported that family in naming, owning, even embracing the Great White Elephant™ for all that it is, as opposed to continuing to ignore it in the hope that it goes away? What if succession planning and wealth transition advisors, perhaps even their whole profession, shifted their focus from the "top of the table" planning—which deals with the *valuables* of a family's wealth—in favor of first dealing with their Great White Elephants and incorporating the family's *values* in the plan?

If such a switch in approach and emphasis were to happen, what would the outcome look like for the client families and the professionals that serve them? Well, certainly it would be a bit more anxiety provoking, since both advisor and clients would have to be willing to address the unspoken feelings and unaddressed issues which exist as emotional undercurrents below the smooth surface of the table top. The proverbial Great White Elephants would have to be brought into the light and fully discussed.

There are five distinct components to a conversational process that when applied to a succession planning and wealth transition process will greatly reduce its chances of failure. Collectively, these five components are what represent "Best Practices" in those families we have had the privilege of serving. When these five steps are taken and fully implemented, the rate of success with the succession planning and wealth transition process greatly increases for you and your family since *values* as well as *valuables* have been taken into consideration.

The five components are:

1. Clarity
2. Congruency
3. Connection
4. Conversations
5. Commitment

Throughout the book, I will give you examples of how each of these component steps are critical to the successful implementation of a business succession and wealth transition plan. In addition these steps will bring you and your family closer together. Emotionally, socially, and economically speaking, you will be a stronger, more congruent, cohesive and successful unit.

There's also the whole matter of values clarification. Might as well include that aspect in our early discussions. To try and simplify the importance of values clarification is perhaps to see them as concepts we all strive to reach, meet, or achieve. Collectively, what we say or name as our values, are also a way of living and holding ourselves accountable. Getting clear on our values involves us letting go of any preconceived ideas of how one is supposed to live one's life, and then living it from a set of predetermined guiding principles, ones values. In the arena of succession planning and wealth transition, this means that inter-generationally, everyone has to get clear on everyone else's values because they shift from one generation to the next; maybe in some areas, the apple never falls far from the tree, but if you never have the conversations, you never get to clarify either areas of convergence or areas of divergence, and then you'll never know where you are in alignment or how far apart you are over the things that matter. Without this sort of clarity on values, you'll never be able to develop any sort of successful strategy for bridging gaps and differences, or finding areas of alignment from which to create any sort of robust structure upon which to plan for family business/enterprise succession, the transitioning of wealth, or anything else that is part of the traditional, technical "top of the table" financial planning process.

It is in defining what matters most to you, and aligning your intentions for the transfer of your wealth, along with the strategies for that transference, in such a way that you actually achieve what it is you want to achieve, based on your values, dreams, and desires for yourself and the next generation. All the while….

Great White Elephant:™ *Why Rich Kids Hate their Parents* is intended to help you realize the importance of a period of reflection and contemplation so you can clearly define what matters most to you. It is the process and means by which you will achieve clarity over what it is you want your wealth to accomplish for your children and their children. It is important that you develop your own rituals around having conversations with yourself and with your children from a values-based perspective. Establish some simple rules or protocols that collectively ensure everyone can depart from any interaction feeling fully acknowledged, heard, and understood. As if this were not already a tall order, you must also have the commitment to live your life authentically—openly, honestly, and congruently, so that you might manage the wealth transition process in such a way that it has the impact you most earnestly desire. To that end, you must also ask what sort of impact do you want your wealth to have upon the generations to come?

This book includes stories about me, the clients I serve in my private practice, and my friends. I hope you will see some of yourself somewhere in these stories. I hope the stories themselves will inspire and challenge you to forge a whole new perspective on how you will approach succession planning and the transfer of wealth. In addition, I hope you will encourage your professional advisors to be more human and apply some emotional intelligence, as they support and guide you in a direction that enables you to deal with the undercurrent issues and emotions that do reside under your table.

Great White Elephant:™ *Why Rich Kids Hate their Parents* is designed to be a working book. While it may be little in size, my intention is that the end result of your reading it will stay with you for a long time. My intention is that you reflect upon the concepts and ideas presented in these pages. Try some of them out. If they don't fit for you, let them go; what fits could assist you in dealing with the Great White Elephant™ in your family. Maybe, just maybe, you will also succeed in developing an open, lasting, and unreservedly loving relationship with yourself and your children.

1

MY GREAT WHITE ELEPHANT: THE OWNERSHIP MYTH

Self-respect knows no considerations.
— MAHATMA GANDHI —

Jake's Great White Elephant™

Money often costs too much.
— RALPH WALDO EMERSON —

JAKE IS A SECOND-GENERATION FAMILY BUSINESS OWNER. His father started the family business by purchasing apartment buildings and later moved into acquiring commercial and industrial real estate. Over a period of about sixty years Jake's father accumulated a portfolio that is now worth in excess of $600 million.

When Jake's father passed away, the shares of the company were passed to both Jake and his two sisters. Having said that, the running of the family business was passed on to Jake's nephew, Blair. Blair had worked closely with his grandfather for about

20 years and, as a result, was entrusted with the running of the family business.

Jake may be 72 years old but when it comes to his emotional maturity over being wealthy, he possesses about the same acumen as a 20-year-old. This is because Jake has never known or had the experience of handling wealth and, until very recently, Jake was accustomed to a lifestyle afforded by an annual income of $120,000. When the typical estate and succession plan was incorporated, shortly before Jake's father died, Jake, at the age of 70, and his sisters, aged 65 and 60 respectively, each received one third of the shares of the family business worth $600 million. All of a sudden Jake went from an income of $120,000 per annum to being worth about $200 million, without any preparation concerning how he might appropriately handle the responsibility that comes with such wealth.

In working with Jake, taking him through a process we call The Values Conversation in which we assist the client in uncovering their core value and Money Motto,™ (what one believes about money, how one feels and consequently behaves with money), we compared Jake's core value and Money Motto™—to see if his belief/s are supporting or hindering his core value, as they relate to what he declares matters most to him.

Jake's Money Motto was defined as: "Money allows me to keep people safe, and ease any issues I have with others." When we explored the costs or the consequences associated with acting out of one's Money Motto,™ what Jake got clear on was the following:

"The Price I pay for my Money Motto™ is that I work on the assumption that money cures all problems, and therefore I don't have to get emotionally involved."

In examining Jake's Money Motto™ reward or the benefits it has for him—and there is usually both a positive and negative side to this—what came up for Jake was as follows:

"The positive reward is that I don't have emotional stress and don't have to get involved in financial decisions.

The negative reward is that I am not as involved as I *need* to be in certain close intimate relationships such as that with my son."

In addition to examining one's Money Motto,™ the price paid for the behavior, and the rewards and penalties for it, the process also involves exploring and identifying whether one's Money Motto™ either empowers or limits how a person deals with money from an emotional perspective as it relates to their core value. Furthermore, we take a look at how one's Money Motto™ has an impact on the individual owner of the motto and the relationship they have with themselves and others who are either members of their family or a close member of their social or business network.

Jake became aware of the limiting nature of his Money Motto™ and how it influences his behavior with money. He realized his tendency is to throw money at problems in his life, and this behavior does not usually do much to actually resolve the problems. When examining how his Money Motto™ impacts his relationships, here's what was revealed for Jake:

- *With himself*: "I use money to try and make problems go away, except I tend either to exacerbate the original problem or end up with more problems than I had at the beginning.
- *With his son*: "I am creating a spoiled brat."
- *With how he handles money*: "I am completely unconcerned. This is because I have only had three years experience in handling significant money and wealth."
- *With his family business*: "I have put the company at risk."

What Jake is referring to is a promissory note he signed in which he pledged his corporate shares as collateral on a loan he guaranteed. He did all this without the knowledge of any of his executive team, which includes his nephew Blair, the current CEO. Jake's action could have proven disastrous for the family business.

I am happy to share that this issue has been resolved, thanks to Jake's executive team and their involvement in the matter once Jake found the courage to disclose his actions. Jake now has a member of the executive team who handles all of Jake's financial affairs—essentially to protect Jake from himself.

This an example of a Great White Elephant™ as it relates to ownership. Here is a clear example of why one must be prepared—both intellectually and emotionally—to become an owner of wealth and be enabled to take appropriate responsibility for it, regardless of your age or stage of life when you inherit.

What's Missing in Transition?

A man who carries a cat by the tail
learns something he can learn no other way.
— MARK TWAIN —

Whenever my professional coaching advice is sought by a business-owning family to assist them with the process of succession planning and/or the transfer of wealth to the next generation, they usually begin by telling me what they have done or are in the process of doing. The conversation usually provides me with a summary of the quantitative work they have thus far accomplished. The quantitative work is what usually gets done first in the traditional approach, in this sort of financial advisory arena. This is perhaps because it is relatively easy to accomplish compared to the emotional piece, since it is a technical, logical, rule-bound process, the outcomes or results of which can be more easily measured or quantified.

The "top of table" work is often undermined, either in whole or in part, by the Great White Elephants living under the table. When I refer to the Great White Elephant,™ I am speaking about all of the unspoken feelings, emotions, and issues in families that are ignored and avoided and never openly brought up for discussion. All families have incidents, events, issues, and topics that they tend to ignore or avoid—their proverbial baggage and skeletons in the closet! This is the baggage that everybody knows about—or thinks they do—over which no one is willing to initiate the often-difficult process of conversation that might actually lead to a clearing of the air, and some collective sense of resolution.

This book is about the new and emerging component of succession planning and wealth transition, which is called the qualitative component.

The qualitative component deals with the emotional and unaddressed aspects of ownership, power, and money. How an individual feels about such dynamics as ownership, power, and money has a significant impact on their relationships with others. What each of us believes to be true about money, and how we deal with money based on our feelings about it is going to affect our relationships with our family, friends, work colleagues, clients—everyone around us. The qualitative component of any business succession planning and wealth transfer process is also going to have to address intra-family relationships and the individual feelings each member of a family unit has about ownership, power, and money, as well as how those individual feelings govern their behavior with every other family member. Yet another aspect of the discussion will be to uncover how each family member feels about the family business, and the historic or long-term impact the running of the business might have on each member of the family—for children, especially so during their formative years, as well as during adolescence and young adulthood.

My experience has led me to conclude that most of the feelings and emotions you will need to address have an associated Great White Elephant™ lurking in the background, or under the table. Great White Elephants are usually strongly felt feelings, unresolved emotions or opinions, about some family issue, event, or topic that has long been avoided and is always evaded during discussions because the long-held, universal perception is that the matter will be to difficult or uncomfortable to deal with and near-impossible to resolve. Here's a list of some of the more common Great White Elephants in individuals and families:

- lack of forgiveness for oneself or others
- anger towards oneself or others
- resentments towards oneself or others
- unclear with oneself regarding love and deservedness
- unspoken expectations of oneself and others
- regret
- guilt
- shame

To return for a moment to the "top of the table" analogy, as a fair description for the quantitative component of any succession planning or wealth transfer process, then the qualitative component represents the under frame and the legs of the table. For the tabletop discussion (the quantitative plan or strategy for bequeathing the wealth or business) to succeed, the under frame and legs have to be strong enough to support it all, otherwise, the table will collapse because the Great White Elephants have not been addressed. As a client of mine so succinctly put it: "Great structures; broken families."

Have you ever stopped and asked yourself why the rate of success for succession planning within a family business from first to second generation ownership is only about 30%?

Most families of wealth are surrounded by the best minds they can find (lawyers, accountants, bankers, investment and risk management advisors) in their respective professions and disciplines. So, why then are the results so poor when it comes to succession planning and the transfer of wealth?

It is my contention that this low rate of success is largely due to the complete lack of attention that is paid to dealing with the Great White Elephants within these business-owning families. I also believe that there are two parties accountable for such poor results in succession planning and wealth transfer situations. The first party is the family itself. More often than not, they all know about the issues they need to deal with. Most always, families are aware of the proverbial "white elephant" in the room, and yet human nature is about avoiding issues that can resurrect old wounds, and create conflict. Stock responses I've heard, all too many times include: "It is too much to deal with right now; I don't want to go there; we can't handle this right now." As a dear friend, Thelma Box, once said: "If nothing changes, nothing changes!"

The second party I hold accountable for this poor success rate are the majority of professional advisors. For the most part they witness and are thus aware of what their clients are struggling with, yet they do nothing of consequence to intervene. The more astute among them may even be able to name the Great White Elephant™ on behalf of a client family. When I've asked some of my professional colleagues and associates, the typical response or excuse for inaction is that they don't know what questions to ask, or that to do so is not their role or mandate. However, when asked or challenged to be more honest with themselves, they will say that they are afraid of upsetting their clients or that the client might get angry with them.

While I might be disappointed by these answers, I am not out to blame anyone in particular or make others feel like they have done wrong. To be fair, many professional advisors are probably feeling out of their depth because they have had no training or experience in managing the qualitative, emotional component of succession planning and the transfer of wealth.

What I am intending to achieve here, is to raise awareness about the current landscape of this profession and propose a new way of dealing with the process of succession planning and the transfer of wealth. One can conduct this process the right way, simply by having the right conversations. You do this by first looking for and then identifying the Great White Elephants for your clients. Once found and identified, you move forward by dealing with all that the Great White Elephants represent and prevent (while they are still in the room) in an effective, caring, and respectful manner.

The Psychic Accountant

Don't let the tax tail wag the emotional dog.
— ALAN LARY —

I would like to tell you about my friend and personal tax accountant, Alan Lary. Alan has figured out how to have the right conversations with his clients, and conduct them in the right fashion. I call Alan the Psychic Accountant. We have served many families together and assisted with the planning and execution of their wealth transition to the next generation. What makes Alan so capable at what he does as well as how he does it is because he has recognized the need to engage his clients in what really matters to them.

I felt this point was so important to share with you, that I interviewed Alan. I asked him to share his opinions with me about what he feels is not working in his profession and how he sees most of his peers deal with their clients. Alan shared that the current approach in focusing on the structural, technical, and financial issues—instead of really understanding the underlying emotional issues at play—is really not working very well for anyone. He claims that most advisors don't understand the "why" before they give advice and implement the technical aspects. Alan also feels the industry is driven by profits and billings, and advisors don't see the potential harm they are doing by putting the structural, technical, and financial issues first. He says the professional advisor needs to be aware of the true issues (Great White Elephants) and understand their client's feelings. They also need to be more patient with their clients, and not be so fast to implement the structural, technical, and financial aspects of any plan.

So, I asked Alan, how do you do this for your clients? His response was to tell me that he had spent time examining his own life. He looked back at what had made him operate the way he had, at what had made him feel what he felt and, as a result, how he had behaved in the past. As Alan says, "All this introspection gave me insight into myself and others and opened me up to considering the wider possibilities and explanations for why others live and operate the way they do."

When asked what it is that clients are looking for in their professional advisors, Alan feels they are looking for the development of effective, tax-structured planning and full tax compliance with those plans. In addition, what clients are also really seeking, but are not willing or able to articulate, is how to develop joy and balance in their lives, how to create truly meaningful relationships with people that are important to them, and to find a way to heal their pain and suffering (resolve and release their Great White Elephants).

Alan asks his clients what is going on in their lives. He asks questions about how they spend their time, what do they focus on, and what's important to them. He also looks to assess the quality of all of the important relationships, regardless of whether they are business-related or family-related. Alan also helps his clients focus on clarifying "why" they are doing what they are doing. He encourages them to participate in a variety of personal development programs, and seek out some personal coaching wherever it is appropriate. Alan also challenges his clients on the results they achieve, both in business and in their personal lives—from a quality-of-life perspective—and explores whether they are capable and willing to do more.

I asked Alan to tell me a little bit about the sort of results he has been seeing and what his clients are achieving as a result of engaging with him in this process. His response:

"There is some discernibly greater momentum in his client's lives, which is characterized in their self-reported feelings of renewal, greater engagement, and excitement about life in general, more energy, a deeper level of joy, as well as an upswing in their financial situation; some report an increase in their legacy and impact on society commensurate with the gains and improvements they have made in their products, services, and relationships."

When I asked Alan what he thought other professionals could do and what advice he might offer them, Al's response was simple, profound, and congruent with the work he has done on himself and on his business practice:

- First, examine your own life so you may gain insight into the lives of others and be in a position to be truly intentional in your work with them.
- Second, the soft issues are paramount.
- Third, don't let the tax tail wag the emotional dog.
- Fourth, be extraordinarily courageous and bold in your advice. Be willing to put your client relationship on the line, if you have to.

I asked Alan to share an instance when he was willing to put his client relationship on the line. He shared the following story with me. He had a mature couple come to him. Both had substantial wealth independent of each other and both owned their own successful businesses. After meeting with Alan, they liked his proposed new structure and the tax advice he gave them regarding the combining of their business interests and assets. They asked him to implement the plan right away. The cost to implement this plan was in the range of $40,000 in fees. Alan asked them to be clear about their relationship and come back only when they could truly commit to remaining in their relationship as a couple. He said he would not implement the plan until they were able to return to him having completed the work that they all agreed appeared to be necessary for their relationship to be strong and healthy for each of them. The couple returned a year and a half later to implement the merger plan.

What is the White Elephant of Ownership?

Getting in touch with your true self must be your first priority.
— TOM HOPKINS —

As a business owner, before you consider a process of succession planning and the transfer of wealth, you must first be clear on your definition of ownership, the different types of ownership, and the Great White Elephant™ so frequently associated with ownership. It is also important to know the extent of the role and responsibilities that are associated with ownership of a business entity or enterprise.

Webster's Dictionary defines ownership as the state, relation, or fact of being an owner. What does it mean to own something? "Belonging to oneself or itself—usually used following a possessive case or possessive adjective," again as defined by

Webster's Dictionary. In the context of a family business or in being faced with accumulated wealth, most of the families I serve in my private practice generally view ownership as both a responsibility and a privilege. While everybody will have their own, slightly different definition for and perspective on what ownership actually means, the tendency we all have as human beings is to settle on a definition of what something means that meets with something close to common if not universal agreement. Achieving some sort of consensus on the meaning of a concept like ownership is an outcome of what I regard as the process of thinking in generalities. I think we do this so that we don't have to take responsibility or be personally accountable for struggling to articulate what ownership actually means to us; we default to a generic definition instead of making it personal—as a product and expression of our own values.

I would like for you to consider ownership from the perspective of your thoughts, feelings, and beliefs. Think about what thoughts are in your head, some of which you have awareness about, but most, I will claim, of which you have little or no awareness. These are your thoughts and you own them too, be they good, bad or ugly. It is these thoughts that will dictate how you feel as an owner, and hence what your beliefs are and, ultimately, what your actions and behaviors are as an owner.

So, the question I ask of you, which is the same one I ask of my own private clients is this: What does it mean to be an owner? In working with Kelly, a second generation family business owner, who is not involved in the day-to-day operations of the business, her definition of being an owner was "to be aware of, but not to be interfering; to be inquisitive about, but not critical or seeking to lay blame." When I asked Kelly how she would have to be or behave to manifest this description of her role, she then responded that she would have to epitomize grace, or act in a graceful fashion. So, Kelly's definition of ownership is to be graceful, to act with grace.

Now, Kelly has not always acted or behaved in a graceful way either as an owner or as a human being. In working together we uncovered Kelly's Great White Elephant™ as a belief about not fitting in, to the extent that she felt she was not really, fully included in the family business, even though she was an owner. As a result of her stated belief of not fitting in, and not feeling included, Kelly admitted this caused her to sometimes behave as a bit of a bully to get her own way over issues and decisions in which she had not initially been included or involved in discussing. This behavior would create tension between herself and her son, who is the current CEO of the family business. Her son felt he had to walk on eggshells whenever his mother would come into the office and he increasingly found that he did not want to include his mother, because of her emotional outbursts and unfounded accusations.

As a result of acknowledging and facing her Great White Elephant™ Kelly was able to see that she was actually perpetrating the very situation about which she was upset and afraid, which was one of being excluded. Once Kelly made the decision to change her view and definition of ownership—to be graceful and act with grace—her attitude and behavior changed. Kelly now approaches situations from a perspective of being genuinely curious and graceful. Today, she has a much closer relationship with her son and his executive team.

If you are a business owner, I would like you to consider that you have a Great White Elephant™ related to that ownership. Consider ownership from the perspective of your thoughts and feelings and, as a result of these, your beliefs. Taking this a bit further, your ownership could be the Great White Elephant™ in your family.

What's Love Got to Do with It?

If you want to be loved, be lovable.

— OVID —

In my conversations with Hal, the owner of a vast family enterprise, he presents this issue in the following way:

"Ownership gives me the opportunity to influence and affect change. With ownership there is also a responsibility towards the people I influence through the decisions I make. There is also a great benefit to ownership through the creation of wealth and the positive impact directly associated with the wealth I create. To be an owner requires fortitude of character, humility, love, and passion for all that one owns. And with this comes great responsibility, not just to what one owns, but to all of those people who are associated with and impacted by what one owns."

His first job, at the age of 12, was sweeping the factory floor on the weekends. At the age of 33, he assumed the helm of his uncle's business (at his uncle's request) and since that time has built it up to a completely different scale and level of profitability.

As a result of working together in a coaching relationship, Hal was able to name and ultimately release his Great White Elephant™ around business ownership. In Hal's case, his Great White Elephant™ was one of regret over not having had the opportunity to work alongside his cousins; regret and a long-standing inability to forgive himself after having been chosen by his uncle—over his cousins—to take over the running of the family business.

Hals' Great White Elephant™ around ownership had been adversely affecting him and the relationships he had with his cousins for quite some time. It also perpetuated the family tendency towards issues of separation and abandonment. This was clearly not what Hal wanted for himself or the family. As a result of going through our initial assessment of what Hal wanted to create as a desired reality for the family, he was able to determine that what he really wanted to do was to create connection, unity, and harmony.

In working with us, Hal was able to identify what his core value was, as one of unconditional love. He also recognized his Money Motto™ (we spend more time discussing the concept and impacts of your Money Motto™ in Chapter 4), which is how he feels about and behaves around money and the impact these feelings have on his relationships, including the relationship he has with himself. Hal named his Money Motto™ as follows: "Money is partly how I show you I love you."

In crystallizing his Money Motto,™ Hal was able to see how his behavior around money limited his ability and freedom to love himself unconditionally, because he uses money as a means of proving to himself that he is lovable. He realized he tended to do this in a more pronounced fashion whenever he was feeling down on himself and in a mental and emotional space of not loving himself. As Hal puts it: "When I get angry or pissed off at myself, I disconnect from myself and use money to buy love."

Hal's Money Motto™ essentially creates a separation and an abandonment of Hal's love for himself because he is using money as a form of self-love, instead of genuinely loving himself unconditionally.

Earlier on, Hal had described what ownership meant to him: "to be an owner requires fortitude of character, humility, love, and passion for all that one owns." What Hal was able to recognize and embrace was that he must first love himself, if he is to love anyone or anything else, let alone his material possessions and financial assets.

In order for Hal to truly and authentically love himself, he had to make the decision to let go of the regret and sadness he carries arising from his uncle's decision to appoint him to run the family business. Hal was able to distinguish the payoff for himself in hanging onto the sadness and regret that he had been so used to carrying around for such a long time. The list included:

- He blames others and does not take responsibility for his role in the situation;
- He gets to be and remain the victim;
- He does not have to hold himself accountable;
- He gets to keep playing small and not living his dream and desire of finding peace and quiet so he can have more time for himself.

In the end, unconditional love has become a cornerstone and a mainstay of Hal's table in his business succession planning process. This has become the emotional component of the plan and has been integrated with the structural, technical, and financial aspects of his plan to transfer wealth to his children.

Today, before Hal makes a decision with his wealth, he asks himself this question:

"How is what I'm about to do, or considering doing, aligned with my unconditional love for myself and those others that matter to me the most?"

Hal's story provides us with a great example of why it's important to get clear on the "why" and implementing it with the structural, technical, and financial aspects of any plan.

As I discussed in my first book, *Life After Wealth:® When is Enough Enough?*, there is a close parallel between how we treat our money and how we treat those closest to us, including how we treat ourselves. In other words money magnifies the core of who we are as individuals, as human beings. If we are naturally kind and generous, money reflects those qualities in us. The converse is also true. If we have a tendency to be controlling and stingy, money will magnify those very same qualities.

It is no different a dynamic with ownership and the power associated with it. When I refer to power I mean the feelings and emotions in the background. One can use their ownership and the power that comes with it for good ends such as business expansion and positive self-expression; it can also be used to control and manipulate others.

Unspoken Expectations are Premeditated Resentments

Love is always bestowed as a gift—freely, willingly, and without expectation. We don't love to be loved; we love to love.

— LEO BUSCAGLIA —

Over the course of the past two decades, since I have been working with family-owned businesses, the most difficult question for any client to answer has been: "What do you want?" It seems that adults have a difficult time in clearly defining, and then seeking out or asking for what they really want. Rather than directly asking for what we want, we often make the request in an oblique and indirect fashion, or we assume that the other person should, by some means, perhaps intuitively, understand our unarticulated desires, wants, and expectations. In other situations, we may refrain from asking for what it is we want out of some concern that our request might not be granted. Not asking means we avoid disappointment and/or a sense of rejection. We may not ask out of a fear of hurting someone else's feelings—because our wants and desires might not match their own (assumptions). In most of these scenarios a process called *scripting* occurs.

Assume for a minute that you are both the author and director of your own dramatic performance. You create a scenario and designate certain roles that you have carefully scripted and choreographed for your players; however, you do not provide the players with your script or give them any overt direction. When the players don't follow the script you have so carefully prepared, you find yourself becoming both frustrated and angry, in spite of the fact that you neither provided the script nor gave any direction. In a situation such as this, you have effectively imposed unspoken expectations upon others without having first clearly communicated to your players what each role entails. When the players subsequently fail to meet your expectations, you feel frustrated and angry with them. Under different circumstances, we might ourselves, assume the role of one of the players. Someone has designated a role for us, but has not shared the expectations they have for us in that particular role. Just as we discussed in the first example, when we do not fulfill the other person's expectations and follow their script, they can feel frustrated and angry.

So, where does the breakdown occur? You took the time to create the script and select the players with care. How could they not know the roles they were assigned to play? The breakdown occurs when communication about expectations is not clear, when we either forget, or overlook the fact that we need to clearly communicate our wants, desires, and expectations and define the roles we want others to play in our particular enterprise. More often than not, it is our failure to communicate clearly which leads to unfulfilled expectations and causes us to feel resentment and misunderstood. The players are usually not at fault because they had no idea there was a carefully constructed script or specific roles they were supposed to be following. Unspoken or unarticulated expectations are really premeditated resentments. We begin to have thoughts like: "this player/person always lets me down, never listens to me, cannot be trusted, or does not understand me." As you are reading this, ask yourself: Who are the key players in your life? How do you treat them? Turning this around: In whose life are you a player? How do they treat you?

In essence, whenever we treat people as players with an unspoken script and little or no direction, or are, ourselves, treated as such, we move into judgment mode. We judge others for not following the script we created, even though we failed to communicate what it is we wanted or would have liked them to do. Unfortunately judgments we make about the performance of others more often than not lead to arbitrary and punitive sanctions arising out of our response to the apparent unwillingness of the players to fulfill the roles and expectations we have planned for them—despite the fact we largely left them in the dark. This lack of communication and the behaviors that inevitably result is ineffective and ultimately dysfunctional and damaging for all.

How do we end up in a position of risking or causing hurt and upset among those players—in a family business, some of those players are members of our family—people who are (or should be) the most important to us both personally and professionally?

Allow me to recap:

1. We had wants, needs, or desires that we did not clearly communicate to the players in our lives and/or in our family business.

2. As a result of our lack of clear communication with our players, we set them up with our unarticulated expectations for achieving our desired outcome—that can never easily be met.

3. When our expectations are not met, we move to a place of resentment.

4. From resentment, we move to judgment and then, in some cases, to punishment.

So, as the author of the script, where does our accountability lie in such a scenario? How can we expect our players to act out our scripts if we have not clearly communicated what we expect or want of them?

Time and again, I have witnessed the negative effects of scripting in family businesses. The older generation often has expectations of the younger generation with respect to their own ethics around work or the perceptions they hold regarding values. (I'll talk more about values in the next chapter).

In a conversation with Mildred, a first generation family business owner, she shared with me how often she feels like she is always running around and doing things for her children, such as picking up her grandkids from school. Mildred is very involved in the lives of her grandchildren, and can do this because she is no longer involved in the day-to-day operations or running of the family business. Her sons now run the business. However, what she has been noticing is that everything she is doing to help her children occurs without any reciprocity. In addition, Mildred realizes that the younger generation believes in a more balanced lifestyle as opposed to focusing on building the business enterprise; Mildred feels this is their opinion because they often acknowledge that the older generation (her generation!) were the ones who built up the business and consequently had little or no time for other things. The younger generation has the luxury of walking into a business which has already been built, and they appear to have the luxury of time to be more balanced and actively seek balance in their lives, unlike their own parents. As a result there will be a different value set as it relates to work-life balance from one generation to the next.

While each of us, as individuals, has a unique perspective on the world, there are also trends among people of the same generation. The perspectives held by one generation then, are going to be different from those held by another younger generation. Speaking in general terms, our elders—parents and grandparents—expect us to understand and follow their lead that has, in most cases, proven to be successful. When a younger generation wants to do something in a different way and they seek to bring their own ethics, values, and perspectives to change the way things have been done in the past, unless these differences in ethics, values, and perspectives are successfully communicated between members of different generations, intended outcomes are not likely to be successfully achieved.

The older (sometimes founding) generation will have an expectation of what ownership means, what it looks like, and how things should be done. By having an expectation of what ownership means and looks like and not clearly communicating this, they are effectively feeding a Great White Elephant,™ (their unspoken expectations around ownership). They will also have a perspective on the responsibilities associated with ownership and whether the next generation is suitably prepared to assume the role of ownership. Some families I have worked with will have a clearly defined set of criteria which outline what they feel is required of a family member to have accomplished or completed before actively joining the family business. More often than not these criteria are quantitative in nature.

An example of this would be the qualifying criteria in the Farnsworth family where any family member who wishes to join the family business must have completed high school with a GPA of at least 3.5, attended and graduated from a University with a degree in business or in a subject area which is relevant to running a business—such as accounting, law, or marketing, and have subsequently worked in a business enterprise similar to their own family enterprise for a minimum of 5 years. After having gained five years of similar work experience, they then qualify to apply for a position within their own family business.

Everyone joining the company starts in a menial position and works their way up the ladder.

Phil's Story:
A Father's Great White Elephant™ Over His Son

Responsibility Educates.
— WENDELL PHILLIPS —

I met Phil for the first time during a workshop I was leading for family-owned businesses. The majority of the group had entered their family business as members of the second-generation in leadership roles. The personal histories of most of these individuals were remarkably similar: their father and /or mother had started a family business, of which they—as son or daughter—had now assumed control, often as the chief executive officer. This was true for Phil, but there was something else about Phil that set him apart from the group. He had an aura, coupled with a meticulous attention to his personal appearance—from the color of watchband to the color of his shoes. As the day unfolded, it was clear that Phil was the individual most respected by rest of the group; they looked to him as a model for financial success, due in large part to the degree of success he had been able to achieve since taking over for his father. Regardless, there was something about Phil that was not congruent with the image he portrayed. Something about Phil was amiss.

A few weeks before my workshop with Phil's group, I was having coffee with my friend and mentor Ken. I told Ken about the workshop I was leading for a group of CEOs of financially successful family businesses. As Ken and I talked, we realized that most CEOs are successful because they are accustomed to being in control of their businesses, which in turn is a form of power. After realizing this we were faced with a question: "How do you take away a CEO's control in such a way that they are unable to control the outcome of a situation? Then, how do you restore their control so that the individual can make the necessary adjustments to achieve what they want based on what really matters to them?" We arrived at the conclusion that the CEOs would have to experience a metaphorical death, and a subsequent re-birth, which would offer them a second chance.

Shortly after entering the room at the beginning of the workshop Phil attended, I turned to the group and said the following words: "I'd like each of you to consider that you have just died." I then asked each CEO to consider, in the event of their own untimely death, what would happen to other key individuals in the family business, and who would they be leaving behind, and record these thoughts on piece of paper. Naturally this exercise led to a discussion concerning their children (the next generation) and the roles that each of those children played in their respective family businesses. The group spent a considerable amount of time discussing whether the children (most of whom were in their mid- to late-thirties) were ready to take on and take over the reins of running the family business. What was interesting in their conversation about readiness was the fact that none of the groups could clearly define or articulate what being ready meant! When asked, each CEO was unable to list with any clarity and certainty how they would know if and when their heirs would be ready. Each CEO spoke candidly about his or her worries and fears regarding the adequacy of business succession preparation their children had received in the event of the unexpected death of a parent who also just happened to run the family business. Two of the wealthiest individuals in the room—one of whom was Phil—came to the realization that unless they made significant changes regarding how they further educate themselves and their children about money and wealth, and what it means to be an owner and all of the responsibilities associated with helming that ownership, they would be all but ensuring the premature demise of the family business and, ultimate, the family unit.

Faced with this realization, Phil began to talk about his son and the high expectations he held for him in spite of his judgments that his son was lazy and appeared unwilling to work hard. As Phil continued to share his frustration surrounding his son's questionable work ethic, one of Phil peers interrupted and asked him what efforts he had made to develop a strong and disciplined work ethic in his son. Here is what Phil's Great

White Elephant™ exposed: his lack of effort and time spent with his son discussing what a work ethic was and what it has meant to Phil's family, and what such a work ethic had created. The question appeared to take Phil off guard. After a short pause and reflection, Phil began to share that he felt his own work ethic had come from his father, the founder of the family business. Not having his question answered, Phil's peer did not relent, and pursued the matter again asking, "How much time do you spend with your son teaching him and talking about what matters most to you, work ethic being one of them?" In other words how are you engaging in conversations regarding your core values and what really matters? Phil was stunned. As he gathered his thoughts and feelings, Phil realized that he had desires and expectations of his son he had not expressed. Phil made the connection that he had been focusing his attention on the unrealized and unarticulated expectations he had of his son and, as a result, he had been living with a deep sense of resentment over what he viewed as his son's laziness. Phil had fallen into the trap of scripting.

Examining this situation from an outsider's perspective, we must ask the question: What is Phil's accountability and responsibility in this situation? I am of the opinion that Phil has a responsibility to invest time in teaching his son discipline and the family's work ethic, rather than focusing solely on the operations of the business and making more money. Phil's story is a perfect example of how a lack of communication, unarticulated desires and expectations that we hold for our children can lead to resentment and divisive relationships in families. This situation is an example of how Phil's unspoken expectations of his son were Phil's Great White Elephant™ within his family. In some cases (such as Phil's) the resentment can lead to judgments that, in turn, can lead to emotional punishment. When an individual moves to a place of emotional punishment they cease to behave in a rational way. One of the greatest mistakes family-owned businesses make is ignoring the need for clear communication and the expression of each individual's desires and expectations. Every member of the family group needs to get clear on their own perspective, be able to communicate that perspective with everyone else in reciprocal fashion, all while maintaining a strong commitment to the integrity of the family as a whole and as an economic, working group.

So, when faced with the need to initiate a succession planning or wealth transition process, or even if you are in the midst of both right now, stop and clarify your intentions. Do this for yourself, your children, and your wealth. Ask yourself this critical, clarifying question: "Are my values aligned with my valuables?"

You might also want to ask yourself and those closest to you, what is the Great White Elephant™ in your family, as it relates to the role of business ownership. What is the nature of the Great White Elephant™ and where does it reside in your ownership structure and/or in how you view or perceive ownership? Do this from your own perspective as well as from the perspective of the next generation who will have to deal with the ownership you bequeath to them.

It is important to realize that Great White Elephants do not always have to be about big decisions or key issues. Great White Elephants can take up residence because of a short, but significant missing conversation, some misperception of one sort or another, a negative thought or pattern of difficult behavior, any of which, if not addressed and dealt with in a timely fashion, have the tendency, over time, to morph into more serious issues.

Over time, small and seemingly insignificant issues which are consistently ignored or remain unaddressed do have a way of becoming Great White Elephants, especially if they are not openly acknowledged and amicably resolved. Ultimately, if a family or business enterprise ends up with a backlog of unresolved issues, this toxicity has a way of putting everything you have worked for at risk. To avoid such catastrophic losses, you must find the courage to face and address your Great White Elephants before they fill the room!

Questions to Ponder...

1. What's missing in your transition plan/strategy?

2. What does ownership mean to you?

3. What kind of owner are you?

4. What kind of owner would you like to be?

5. What is your Great White Elephant™ as it relates to ownership?

2

VALUES AND VALUABLES

*The human race has had long experience and a fine tradition
in surviving adversity. But we now face a task for which
we have little experience, the task of surviving prosperity.*

— ALAN GREGG —

The Values Conversation: The Why

*Men go abroad to wonder at the heights of the mountains,
at the huge waves of the sea, at the long courses of rivers,
at the vast compass of the ocean, at the circular motions of the stars,
and yet they pass by themselves without wondering.*

— SAINT AUGUSTINE —

THINK OF A CONVERSATION ABOUT VALUES as what is needed for you to effectively deal with your Great White Elephant™ so that it no longer remains a burden for you or that it remains one you pass on to the next generation. Values and your clarification of them is what will provide you with stability when the Great

White Elephant™ is running amok. Think of your values as the legs of a table that will hold the structural, technical, and financial issues of the wealth transfer and succession plan in place. By first identifying and clarifying your own (individual) values, and later those of everyone else in the family, values provide a framework and become tools to manage the Great White Elephants whenever they show up (become apparent). It is only by putting values first and clarifying what they are, that you can eventually identify your Great White Elephants in relation to your values and realize that it has more to do with the management of your values, and acting in congruence with them, as opposed to the structural, technical, and financial positioning of your valuables or assets.

What's important about money to you? This seems like a simple question to ask. On one level, it is, but for anyone to answer it honestly takes courage and a willingness to reflect on what truly matters to us in our own life. In my experience, people think they know what matters to them, and deep down maybe we do, but we are often unwilling to examine and face up to the gap between our values and how we live by the values we espouse. All of us don't always walk our talk, then, and some of us may have a Great White Elephant™ to deal with, with respect to our values perspective that we may not be willing to look at or address. There is nothing unusual about this sort of human predicament. It's more a matter of deciding what action you are willing to take to bridge the gap.

More often than not, what we do with our time and money has little or no bearing on what really matters to us. In fact, taking a critical look at both our calendar and our checkbook would reveal how large the gap is.

It is our lack of clarity about what matters to us that creates the gap. In lacking clarity, we make assumptions about what matters to us, as opposed to knowing with certainty what actually matters to us. Once we are clear, we can operate with congruency, where our talk becomes our walk. What we say and what we do become one and the same. When one operates from this platform, there is a connection between the two and this becomes the foundation of the "why." Now one is driven by the "why," simply because of the congruency, and one does things and behaves a certain way that is in alignment with ones stated values.

For example one does not do things to be compassionate, one is compassionate and hence acts a certain way. In this example, the "why" is compassion.

The "Why" is Foundational!

It doesn't matter about money; having it, not having it.
Or having clothes, or not having clothes.
You're still left alone with yourself in the end.
— BILLY IDOL —

In the succession planning and wealth transition industry, the question that most frequently arises is over how the valuables will be bequeathed and disbursed to the next generation. Advisors spend significant amounts of time with clients exploring the best strategies for wealth transference with a view to protecting and preserving the wealth, safeguarding and enhancing its monetary value, and managing the legal and tax implications. It is important to point out, that in most cases the client isn't initially clear on what their "why" is. In my experience, this is the reason why most business succession plans and wealth transfers fail. The structural, technical, and financial aspects of the planning have not been based on the "why" (the "why" behind their decision to bequeath the valuables in the first place). Advisors surely need to know the technicalities to do their job in a competent fashion, but they first need to know something of the mind, heart, and soul of their clients—both the benefactor/s and beneficiaries of the wealth under review.

Knowing the answer your client would give to the question of why they are bequeathing their wealth should really be the first order of business and, if any planning for business succession or wealth transfer is going to be congruent with client values, then knowing the answer or reasons "why" is critical to any advisor's ability to plan "how" the succession planning or wealth transfer will actually be executed. I want to remind you of Al's story in Chapter 1 and the success and impact he is having with his clients as a result of his getting to know the "why" as he assists his clients to clearly articulate their reasons "why." I would like to again acknowledge Bill Bachrach and his work in developing and teaching me the simple and profound technique for guiding a values-based conversation. His book, *Values-Based Financial Planning: The Art of Creating an Inspiring Financial Strategy* is one I highly recommend for those who wish to engage in this process with their own clients.

The premise of Bill's work, and now my own, is that when people understand the emotional drivers behind their wealth accumulation and ultimately their wealth transfer, they have clarity, motivation, and commitment to take their transition plan seriously and enroll their advisors and their children in the "why," that is, their values. Values are the emotional links (legs of the table) that can make all the difference to the long-term success of any succession plan and wealth transfer process.

The challenge that most people have however, and this is often the source of one of their Great White Elephants, is that they are not clear on what their values are—they do not know or understand their reason/s "why." This is an example of a Great

White Elephant,™ not knowing one's "why." Values are essential for any client family to clarify so that they might effectively deal with the Great White Elephant™ their valuables represent; values-clarification can ease the burden of succession planning and the transfer of wealth.

Values are defined as a collection of guiding, usually positive principals, which one deems to be proper and desirable in life, especially regarding one's personal conduct.

So, what are the valuables? The ownership, the money and the power associated with ownership and money. Think of the role and status of ownership, money, and the power each can wield as one of the Great White Elephants that reside in wealthy families. Given over too early and without proper emotional and mental preparation, wealth, ownership, and power can become a tremendous burden for the recipient.

The challenge is that parents (those holding and planning on bequeathing the wealth) will operate out of their own notion of what ownership means, from both a conceptual as well as an emotional perspective. They will do the same with power and money. Holding onto a different perspective and having a different meaning for ownership, power, and money obviously makes the business succession plan and wealth transition process difficult if one cannot be clear about the meaning of these fundamental concepts. With a lack of clarity on what ownership, power, and money mean—no universal understanding—there are bound to be unspoken or confused desires and expectations that will be attached to what the next generation must do with the ownership, power, and money and how the benefactors are supposed to behave—all based on the assumption that everyone knows, understands, and perhaps even shares the same ideas.

Such assumptions as these are a Great White Elephant™— one arising from a lack of clarity! A parent might have a certain way of behaving as an owner, and hence they will unconsciously expect their children to behave in a similar fashion when it comes to their becoming the succeeding owner. This is especially true when those who stand to inherit and assume ownership are assuming responsibility for something their parent/s built— which is, by extension, simply a reflection of who they are and all that they have stood for. There are three main reasons why most founders of family businesses struggle to let go of the reins from an emotional perspective:

- *The transition of ownership results in a loss of identity*: outside of the role of business founder, owner or leader, they have no clear idea of who they are.
- *The transition of ownership results in a loss of purpose*: outside of the role of business owner, founder, or leader, they have no clear idea how they can any longer make a meaningful contribution.
- *The transition of ownership disrupts some fundamental version of the business founder's Money Motto™*: (e.g., making money gives me power, or money buys me respect).

I am of the opinion that it is imperative for the current owners of a business enterprise to get clear on the meaning they attach to ownership, power, and money, particularly from an emotional perspective. Once they have clarity, they will be able to bequeath their ownership, power, and money in way that is congruent with their values. They will also be able to communicate this clarity and their values to the members of the next generation as well as their team of financial advisors. This approach will help create the required common platform of understanding, first for the current owner/s with and between themselves, and then between one generation and the next. It is from here that a family will have the commitment to stay the course based on the clarity of values and the emotional meaning associated with ownership, power, and money.

Here again is a list of emotional Great White Elephants that will play out and have an impact upon how one views ownership, power, and money, based on the meaning one attaches to these.

- lack of forgiveness for oneself or others
- anger towards oneself or others
- resentments towards oneself or others
- unclear with oneself regarding love and deservedness
- unspoken expectations of oneself and others
- regret
- guilt
- shame

These Great White Elephants have to be acknowledged and addressed before the top of table work—the structural, technical, and financial issues of the wealth transfer and succession planning—can occur and if it is to be truly successful and sustainable for future generations.

We've already stated in general terms how it is that professional advisors whose focus is on succession planning and wealth transition nearly always begin with a top of the table conversation about the "how's" part of the process. In most cases the "how" is figured out and based solely on the current owner's perspective. More often than not, the perspectives of the benefactors, the individuals from the next generation for whose benefit this plan is being designed, are never sought out in a parallel conversation or taken into account in any meaningful fashion. The "how's" are nearly always based on technical issues, without any consideration given to the implications—never mind the emotional impact—the plan might have for the inheriting members of the next generation.

Walking Through the Wall of Guilt

*"The practice of forgiveness is our most important
contribution to the healing of the world."*

— MARIANNE WILLIAMSON —

I recall meeting Victor, a second-generation family business
owner. At our first meeting, Victor told me without any desire
to cause offence: "Franco, I already have a team of advisors
helping me with my succession plan, so why do I need you?" My
answer was very simple and direct—Perspective! Victor was busy
developing his succession plan for his children, and doing it all
without consideration for their views or perspectives on the plan
or its future emotional impact on any of them.

Victor has three sons (aged 36, 32 and 26). One of his stated
concerns is over how his children will work together as a team.
Do they want to? Are they capable of doing so even if they want
to? Are there any unresolved issues—sibling rivalries—between
his sons of which he has little or no knowledge, that could prevent
them from working together as an effective management team?
Are there any Great White Elephants that need to be identified
and resolved between Victor and his three sons?

It was my hope and expectation that the answers to all these
questions, and more, had to be addressed before Victor got much
further down the road with his current advisors. If not, the "top

of the table" discussion and technical succession plan stood a significant chance of failing.

Unlike most men of his generation, Victor had separated and divorced and, for a period of almost 20 years, lived without remarrying. Now happily remarried and with two much younger children, currently aged 7 and 4, the issue that kept Victor awake at night was how he was going to bequeath his assets equitably among his five children—three much older children from his first marriage and the two youngsters from his second. How does one equitably divide assets among five children from three very different, entirely unrelated business enterprises?

Having said this, dividing his assets among five children was not the most significant Great White Elephant™ in Victor's world. During the years Victor was married to his first wife, he was almost exclusively focusing on building the business and took significant time away from his young family at the time to do so. As a result of Victor's investment of time, his hard work paid off, and he doubled the value of the original business passed to him from his father thereby amassing massive wealth. Inevitably, during those years of building his business enterprise, his lifestyle was nowhere near what it is today. Today, his business has a significant value and is highly complex in nature, and his lifestyle reflects this evolution and success.

Victor's Great White Elephant™ relates to the guilt he feels over the limited accessibility he had to his older children, when they were younger, at the time he was consumed with the building of the family business passed down to him by his own father. Now that he has a new, young family, he is torn between the two responsibilities. Victor does not want to make the same mistakes with his two younger children as he made with the children from his first marriage. At the same time, he also desperately wants to make up for lost time with his older children.

In the midst of all of this, Victor is working with his advisors on a plan for the succession of his three business enterprises, and his advisors are diligently dealing with the entirety of the usual "top of the table" issues. Yet Victor and I have now identified this emotional undercurrent and the Great White Elephant™ that, left unresolved, puts all the current "top of the table" planning in jeopardy.

The emphasis of the succession plan to-date has been on figuring out how to divide and bequeath assets to two sets of children with a significant age difference between the two. What does Victor do with respect to ownership? How is that issue to be dealt with? Victor is currently 68, and within the next five years he has stated he would like to retire from being the CEO of his business operations and have his three older children jointly assume that responsibility.

How did Victor address his own Great White Elephants as well as those of his immediate family? How did Victor effectively manage and change the direction of succession planning in such a way to ensure that everyone in his family felt heard, understood, and taken care off? How did Victor release his guilt and manage to transition his business interests and assets in such a way that the valuables were passed on in a way that reflected his values and what mattered most to Victor?

In working together, we identified Victor's core value as one of transparency, which meant for Victor that he is open and honest about what he feels, thinks, and does. This included Victor being transparent with himself about the regret and sadness he has over not being present for his older children while they were growing up. Victor had to see for himself how he had been behaving differently with his older and younger children as a result of caring the burden of sadness and regret. These two burdens were preventing him from first being honest with himself and then with his older, adult children. Victor was trying to make up for lost time, with money, and in passing on the ownership of his vast business empire.

We also identified Victor's Money Motto™ as: "Money is a measure of how I love you." What Victor was doing—at a subconscious level—was using his money as a way to show all of his children that he loved them. He felt that if he divided his assets equally among the five of them, this would show them all that he loved them equally. This had been the strategy his technical team had been trying to figure out, based on Victor's direction, and unidentified Money Motto™.

However this approach was not really getting to the "why" for Victor. Until Victor started working with us, he did not have any clarity over his intentions or his reasons "why!" As it turned out, Victor's "why" is transparency.

Having achieved clarity on Victor's "why" the process we took Victor through was to gain some similar clarity about the impact his Money Motto™ was having on himself, his family, and his business succession plan. We continued coaching Victor until he was able to realize how his lack of transparency had impacted his three older sons, and the succession planning process. The next step was for Victor to find a way to walk his talk from his stated value of transparency, to becoming congruent in his behavior and actions. Victor had to take responsibility for the times he had not been transparent and the negative impact his lack of transparency had caused. Part of being congruent, was being willing to forgive himself for not being there for his older sons, and letting go of the sadness and regret that there are things you cannot go back and fix.

If Victor could find a way to forgive himself and let go of his regret, he would be building a pathway forward to the third step in the process: reconnection. Once Victor was able to forgive himself, he got reacquainted with himself—emotionally and spiritually, and was thereafter able to connect with his older sons at a much deeper level—one which money could not parallel. Victor was able to create a new family environment where he could have deep, rich and meaningful conversations. Ultimately, over time these new conversations became the hallmark of a newly built level of trust and a joint commitment over the future of the family business, in which all adult members of the family participated. This family work became the core content of an eventual working document entitled *Values-Based Wealth Distribution*, which is the true and lasting legacy Victor was able to create with and for his family, by not only being transparent with himself, but in promoting transparency with every member of his immediate family.

Bang! You are Dead!

> *Things which matter most, must never be*
> *at the mercy of things that matter least.*
> — GOETHE —

My belief is that before embarking on the process of succession planning and the transfer of wealth it is important that the reasons "why" be identified and shared with the intended beneficiaries of the plan. Most times, the "why" is hidden behind a Great White Elephant™! Sometimes the family knows the identity of the Great White Elephant,™ sometimes not. Either way, the Great White Elephant™ must be acknowledged, named, and fully discussed.

One approach to initiate a conversation about Great White Elephants is to develop a more gentle, oblique approach to bringing them out in the open so that their owners can see them up close and personal. In Chapter 1, I talked about this concept during the workshop I led for a group of CEO's of family-owned businesses.

I wanted to create a scenario through which they could see how they were presently living life, and describe that present reality, as opposed to how they would actually live their life if everything were based on what really mattered to them most—their core values.

Here's how that workshop unfolded. During the first session, I asked the participants to clearly identify what really mattered to them most, as human beings, as parents, as business owners and, in some cases, as philanthropists. Once they clarified what mattered to them in all of these various roles or positions, we worked through a values-clarification exercise to distill everything to a smaller set of core values like authenticity, integrity, respect, and wisdom; you get the picture. Once this was complete, we asked them to define—with clarity and in practical terms—what their identified core value meant to them as individuals. We did this because a word, such as respect, will mean one thing to you and it might have a totally different meaning to me.

After all the participants had achieved some greater clarity on their values and what they meant, the next step of the workshop asked participants to look at a recent, but typical week of engagements and commitments for themselves, and reflect on that week, and ask themselves one question: "How much time during that week, did I spend time acting in a way that was truly congruent with what I now say is my core value?" For most, the answer was quite an eye opener. This is an exercise you might want to adopt for yourself and see how congruently you actually live your life in terms of living out your stated core values.

During the second session of the workshop, we asked participants to make a list of all of their assets. This list was to include all of the valuables, such as: trusts, real estate holdings, business assets, stock and bond portfolios, yachts, art collections, horses, wine or coin collections—basically any significant material or monetary asset. Once they had made a full inventory, we asked them to look at how their valuables were presently structured and earmarked for future disbursement or transition. For example, if someone had a will that was not complete or was in the process of being amended, then for the purposes of the workshop exercise, we worked with whatever happened to be the real life situation and circumstances for participants at the time.

At this point in the day, we now had the participants with their structured list of valuables, and all having identified and clarified their core value, and I proceeded to kill all of them— bang!, bang!, bang! You are all now dead, metaphorically speaking!

Just as soon as all these CEOs had met with a sudden and untimely death, we brought them all back to life as observers of their own continuing existence. Their role in the next part of the workshop was to reflect upon and then discuss as a group what would have likely happened to their loved ones had they actually met with a sudden and untimely death given the real state of their personal, financial, and business affairs; given the way they were, at the time, living their life?

More than one of the participants got a wake up call over the mess he/she had left their family with—including an unfinished will. Another got to see how his two sons, both in their twenties, were nowhere near prepared to assume responsibility for running the family business, and the impact this lack of preparedness would have on the family, the business, and its employees. Phil, whom I talked about in Chapter 1, gained significant insight into the potential consequences of unarticulated desires. Phil became aware of how his unspoken desires and expectations of his son had contributed to his son's lack of readiness—both experientially and emotionally—to take over for Phil if and when he was no longer around.

The final session of the workshop was probably the most powerful and impactful element of the whole day for these CEOs. We asked each participant to look at how their valuables were structured and if this current state of affairs was lined up with the value they had clarified and defined in the first part of the workshop. Not one individual had their valuables structured in a way that was in alignment with their core value. This was not because the structure was necessarily wrong; it was because their values had not been clearly defined or articulated at the time they applied a structure to their valuables; the two, therefore could never be said to be in alignment.

This realization (misaligned values and valuables) was a Great White Elephant™ for all participant CEOs: the unidentified values and the "why," completely disconnected to the valuables and the "how!" Might I suggest that readers could have a Great White Elephant™ of their own with respect to a misalignment between their values and valuables, and their "why" and their "how"?

What is Love?
The Glue between Why and How

A baby is born with the need to be loved—and never outgrows it.
— FRANK HOWARD CLARK —

Love is one of the most powerful feelings we get to experience as human beings. It can make us feel powerful or weak and insecure all at the same time. Love is one of the greatest motivators of all. Yet when we think of love we all, and this is an assumption on my part based on my personal experience, first think of love in relation to loving another. Until very recently, I have never related to love as loving myself.

In the coaching work we undertake with our clients, a common theme that emerges is the lack of self-love. This lack of self-love typically stems from a place of believing that there's something wrong with you. In the work we do with our clients, we assist them to become more aware of what has occurred in their lives; that is to become more aware of the life-changing moments and experiences, the critical, foundational, and sometimes but not always, traumatic event/s that have transpired. We ask them to try and clarify the meaning they ascribed to those events and the conclusions, assumptions, or judgments they also made about themselves, as a result of what happened.

As a child, I was bullied and as a result of that experience, I attached a meaning to it—which is that I'm not safe or valuable, I am not worthy, and that I don't fit in. I made up these beliefs about myself, and consequently have had a difficult time ever since in accepting myself, let alone loving myself.

As a matter of fact, I didn't know how to love myself. I knew how to love others, but not myself, until recently. Melody Beatty's book of daily meditations, *Journey to The Heart*, of which I have had a copy for years, is a work which I recently found myself revisiting. Today's reading:

Love Yourself Until It's Real

Love is, above all, the gift of oneself.
— JEAN ANOUILH —

What does it mean to love yourself? To do nurturing things for and to yourself? Yes, sometimes. But self-love runs deeper than that. Self-love means loving and accepting yourself, your thoughts, beauty, emotions, your faults, imperfections, and flaws, your strengths, wit, wisdom, as well your peculiar and unique way of seeing the world.

Loving yourself means accepting and loving each and every part of you, and knowing-knowing-that you are worthy, valuable, and lovable. It means loving and accepting yourself when you are surrounded by people who love you, and during those times when you think everyone's gone away, when you wonder if God's gone away too.

Sometimes, loving ourselves means accepting ourselves enough to tell ourselves other people like and approve of us. Sometimes, loving ourselves means approving of ourselves, even when they don't. It takes courage to stop cowering and openly love, accept, and approve of ourselves.

Don't just say the words. Love yourself until you experience that love.

I have read this passage many times, as I have owned *Journey to The Heart* for over a decade. Yet, for the first time, I realize that I don't know how to accept myself, let alone love myself. I have had a number of friends and acquaintances say to me that I need to be kind, generous, and compassionate with myself. All qualities I passionately and freely give to others, particularly those I love.

As a result of a recent personal, intimate, and romantic relationship, I have become more conscious of the fact that when I am in such a relationship, at some point I fall fully and completely in love. What occurs is interesting. I give of myself completely, and keep nothing for myself. What do I give? ... Love, kindness, empathy, time, money, acceptance, forgiveness, and compassion—all that and more.

One would think all of this would be a great gift to the recipient. However, I have come to realize it is actually a burden. Because I have given it all away, there is nothing left in my tank, and as result I start to look towards others, in this case my former girlfriend, for some or all of that which I freely gave away to her. That depth of need can never be fully met by another person, because there is an emptiness that cannot be filled. Over the years, there have been a number of women with whom I have been romantically involved, and I have realized that every one of them has said, at some point in our relationship: "Franco. I cannot seem to satisfy the insatiable need for love you have!"

I see all this now. I am 46 years old, and the next step for me is to not only love and accept myself, but to fall in love with myself. So, what am I learning? In retrospect, as I look back on this most recent relationship that fell apart, I gave her everything, except the one thing that really mattered to her. From the outset of our relationship, she told me that the most important thing in a relationship for her was integrity. Her definition of integrity was "be your word." In my relationship with her, I did not live or act from a place of complete integrity, and thus I did not give her what she most wanted. As a consequence, the relationship ended. What am I learning in all of this? To give relationships what they want and need.

You might be asking yourself what is the point I am trying to make in sharing this story? Firstly, I think we need to be clear on what our relationships want and need from us. We must try not to make assumptions or have desires that remain unspoken or unarticulated, or only operate out of our own perspective. We must strive to take the perspective of others into consideration. We say we love our children or those closest to us, yet we are often not very clear on what they want or need from us—and how we might then express our love to them.

I like to use the analogy of a cup of water. One cannot give a person a drink from an empty cup. So, how can anyone love another person if they don't know how to love themselves? As I shared with Hal's story in the previous chapter and how important it was for him to get clear on the importance of Hal loving himself first, so he had a clear and congruent basis upon which he could then express his love for his children and subsequently take steps to plan for the passing on of his business assets in a way that was in alignment with his core values—the first of which, for Hal, was love. Without love, first for himself, it made it difficult for Hal to unite the "why" with the "how."

The second point is that at our core, we are all searching for love. Most of us, and I include myself here, tend to look for love extrinsically, by buying things, acquiring things or needing to be in a relationship with another to validate our basic need for love. What we realize, over time, is the limitless source of love as an inside job. As we love ourselves, we enhance our capacity to love others.

I have worked with many business-owning families in which the individual family members did not know what their fathers, mothers, brothers, sisters, grandparents, grandchildren, cousins, uncles and aunts wanted and needed from one another. It amazes me that people will be in relationship with each other and yet not know what really matters to the other person, and what the other person wants, needs, and values the most.

Clarity of Vision: What Are You Teaching Your Kids?

*Each day of our lives we make deposits
in the memory banks of our children.*
— CHARLES R. SWINDOLL —

What do you want your life to look like? This is a question I love asking my clients. It sounds easy enough, yet in most cases the answer is very difficult to articulate. Why is this the case? My theory is that most of us have a view that life is hard and that we don't deserve to have either the things we covet or the life we say we want. Or perhaps, when we were young, we might have shared an idea or dream with someone and the way they responded caused us to make a decision that it is ultimately not okay to have dreams—especially the one/s you dared to articulate.

One of the greatest challenges that older generations have is that they don't have sufficient clarity of vision with respect to their own wealth and the desires or hopes they hold for their own children. In some cases the older generation does have an idea of what they want for their children, but it is all framed from their own perspective, and usually they have never directly asked their children what they want and need and hope for (this is a common Great White Elephant™ in numerous families). Furthermore, since money and wealth is more often than not a difficult topic of conversation and therefore one to be avoided (itself a Great White Elephant™) since culturally, at least in WASP culture—white, Anglo-Saxon Protestant culture—it has long been seen as vulgar to talk directly about money and wealth, most families rarely talk about money and wealth, and hence shelter the younger generation from it and all of its implications, both for better and for worse.

Some people who inherit significant wealth and money are able to navigate the transition with very little disruption and emotionally unsettling consequences, and I would argue that this is because they have been raised in a family that habitually has talked about the pros and cons of money and wealth and how each family member feels about it. These people are not as likely to be adversely affected by their money and wealth and can more easily integrate being wealthy and carry the responsibility that wealth brings into their lives with far greater aplomb.

Conversely, there are others who stand to inherit significant wealth, who come from families that did not have those same conversations about money, wealth, or values and are far more likely to inherit with strong feelings of ambivalence around the transition, finding themselves disconnected and confused over their inheritance. Some people who inherit significant money and wealth experience it as a painful transition and can express strong feelings including shame, guilt, low self-esteem, loneliness and even resentment over where or how the wealth was generated.

Most of the rest of society tends to look at rich kids with either a sense of loathing or jealousy, or some combination of the two, assuming that their lives are easy and labels them as spoilt brats or trust fund babies. In her dissertation, *The Experience of Inherited Wealth: A Social-Psychological Perspective*, Joanie Bronfman coined the word *wealthism* and writes:

> "Wealthism includes those actions or attitudes that dehumanize or objectify wealthy people, simply because they are wealthy. The main attitudes of Wealthism are envy, awe and resentment… Wealthism differs from the other "isms" in that racism and sexism are perpetrated by those that have power, whereas Wealthism is directed at those that have power."

Parents have a sense of how this attitude towards wealthy people affects their children, so they try and protect their kids from this. They try to shelter their children while trying to conceal their wealth. For some children this is confusing. The children see how their parents live and participate in their lifestyle, yet the parents might be telling the children to not tell others they are rich. This double mixed messaging can be damaging for the long-term development of kids. They grow up confused, with the messaging that it is not okay to be you, i.e., wealthy. Hence, wealthy children will grow up with the messaging that they must conceal their wealth due to the fear of being stereotyped and bullied by a society that is jealous and envious of the wealthy in general. As a result, some rich kids will start to lie about their wealth. They might say things like: "I can't really afford to go on a holiday with my friends," yet they will be wearing very expensive clothes. This typically leads to what might feel like a double life for some of these kids when they end up going to college.

Billy's first experience with Wealthism occurred when he went to college. Luckily for Billy, his last name was a fairly common name, so he didn't have to worry about his new friends at college recognizing his family name and knowing about their wealth. In a conversation, he shared with me how shocking it was for him to hear his peers openly discuss their jealousy and envy of "those rich people," and how easy it must be to be a "trust fund baby." He made a decision to not share the truth of his background with his new peers. Billy lived in fear that one day, his peers would discover who he really was and the extent of his family wealth. As a result, Billy started to withdraw and became a loner in college.

Why Rich Kids Hate Their Parents

Holding onto anger is like grasping a hot coal
with the intent of throwing it at someone else;
you are the one that gets burned.
— BUDDHA —

In my opinion and experience in working with some of the world's wealthiest families, there are three main reasons that contribute to children hating or resenting their parents and the wealth they have been blessed with (but don't see it as a blessing).

1. Parents general inability to say "no" to their children's requests.
2. Parents trying to make up for lost time or their own feelings of guilt with money. They try to buy their children's love.
3. Parents messaging about what it means to be wealthy and have money.

In an interview with Daniella, a 35-year-old urban designer, we discussed what it was like for her to attend a private school and the impact her family wealth had on her classmates at that time. Daniella attended a posh private school in North Carolina, when her family moved from Europe to the US. She shared how her peers were disconnected from the realities of life as a result of their parent's wealth, and how, in some cases, they were not challenged by the teachers in school because of who they were, i.e., the power attributed to being the offspring of a wealthy family.

There were lots of instances of peer exclusion, all based on the level of wealth one's family had. In addition, there were the inevitable cliques that formed in school and, for Daniella, these divisions were dependent upon whether one came from a family of old money or you were one of the nouveau-riche, or an affluent immigrant family. There were constant comparisons being made between children as a result of the wealth that was flaunted at the school.

A common feeling held by the majority of these "rich kids" was one of frustration, resentment, and anger towards their parents; they also had feelings of neglect, and of not feeling loved by their parents, because their parents were never really around. These kids had nice material possessions, which their parents had bought for them, but most kids didn't really value these things because they knew they were bought as a substitute for attention or affection. As a result, these children would show a remarkable lack of appreciation for their material possessions, most or all of which had been purchased for them by their parents. Lots of kids also behaved in an irresponsible or reckless fashion, either to seek attention or as a cry for help from largely emotionally absent parents.

Daniella recalled that many of her peers would spend weekends or holidays at home alone with all of their new gadgets and toys, feeling abandoned and angry. Lots of valuables, few values and a dearth of the glue that holds it together—*love*.

Daniel is 25-years-old, and the oldest of three sons. At the age of 18, he received a letter from his father—which had been drafted by the family lawyer—that clearly stated what Daniel could expect from his father in terms of future financial support. The letter outlined how much Daniel would receive and what expenses would be covered. In addition, the letter outlined what family recreational properties Daniel had access to and what that access would cost him if he wanted to make use of those properties. The letter also addressed what Daniel could expect in terms of financial support to buy a car (specified makes and models), support for post-secondary education, buying his own home, and how he could get involved in the family business should he choose to do so. The letter detailed how much Daniel could expect to receive—and when—as a down payment on a home of his own. In affect, the letter was formal, impersonal, and had very clear legal overtones.

The impact the letter had on Daniel was not what his father had hoped to achieve, which was to provide structure and clearly outline what Daniel could expect in terms of financial and material support. During our coaching sessions, Daniel recalled the impact his receipt of the letter had had on him, and how it altered his relationship with his father. Since receiving the letter, Daniel shared that he no longer feels safe having conversations with his father regarding money, because he has an "already always listening" experience of his father, that is, he feels he already knows how his father will react in any conversation about money. As a consequence of this letter, Daniel states that he now withholds a part of himself whenever he expresses himself with his father. He does not feel acknowledged or valued or trusted by his father when it comes to "money issues." As a result Daniel feels that his father is not aware of the emotional impact his letter has caused for Daniel, any more than he is aware of the separation that is taking place between father and son.

Now Daniel harbors a deep resentment toward his father, and does not feel safe or comfortable approaching his father to have conversations about financial matters. While the letter he received was clear with respect to the valuables, it did not address anything to do with the "why." All Daniel could see was his father lording over him. As Daniel puts it: "Dad is always trying to control me, and has not given me an opportunity to be responsible with money and clearly does not trust me." This made Daniel very angry, and as a result he stopped talking to his father about anything to do with money. Rather than the letter creating closeness and clarity—which is probably what his father had hoped to accomplish—it has caused separation and anger.

In working with Daniel's father, Craig, we were able to elicit from him the "why" behind the letter. We asked him to recall his original emotional intent and what it was that he really wanted to accomplish with this letter for his son. Craig's Money Motto™ was revealed as: "It's easy for me to make money; hence I don't value or respect it."

What Craig was doing—at a subconscious level—was projecting his Money Motto™ onto his son. By this I mean Craig was assuming that his son would treat his money in the same way and reflect Craig's own beliefs about money. Here's the catch, Craig didn't know with any clarity what his beliefs about money were until we uncovered them. Craig made the assumption that his son Daniel would view money in the same way as he did himself and hence treat it in similar fashion. So, Craig thought, I'll put something in place to protect my son. What he did not consider was his own view about money. He also didn't think to acknowledge or first explore whether his son might have different views or opinions about money.

These blind assumptions were a Great White Elephant™ for both Craig and his son Daniel. Craig's undisclosed and unrevealed Money Motto™ had got in the way of what Craig really wanted to achieve, which was to protect Daniel from becoming like his father (Craig) when it came to his feelings about wealth and his behavior around money.

One of the most common reasons why some rich kids end up hating their parents is because the parents made life too easy for them when they were growing up. It's a double-edged sword. Parents typically accumulate wealth by working hard and following their work ethic. The values of a hard work ethic clearly have a bearing on the accumulation of wealth but when it comes time to plan for the transition of that wealth, one must look at a different set of values. As I often say, it's the values that create the valuables; but it is not necessarily the same values that facilitate the wealth transition.

Working hard, and putting in the time to build a successful business, usually means long hours away from family that always and only ever comes at a price. The price is typically one of time away from family events and activities, missing out on so many important milestones; sometime missing out on seeing your children grow up. Parents who do this are making a deal with themselves—at least at a subconscious level. The deal is that once they have accumulated wealth and have attained a certain level or quality of lifestyle and they are providing for their family in the way they have long, or always envisioned, they will make it (time away) up to their family. I call this guilt.

Once the parents are in a position to begin to pay off the debt of guilt—one that they have been carrying for years, perhaps decades—they do so in the only way they can, which is financially, and some of them soon realize that money is not the same currency as time, guilt, or shame. One cannot make up for lost time by writing a check. The parents want to make up for lost time or assuage their guilt so, in most cases, they make life easy for their children and do this without every realizing that this is what they are perpetrating. The rationale most parents use is that they don't want their children to suffer in the same way they did themselves. In doing so, the parent unintentionally and without realizing it, undermines the natural ambition and initiative for their own space, power, and autonomy that all children possess—which ironically, are some of the very same human attributes that helped the parents generate (or accumulate) the valuables and wealth in the first place.

Another likely reason for rich kids hating their parents can arise out of a child's need to conceal the family wealth as I discussed in a previous section of this chapter. The child grows up with the belief that it is neither okay nor particularly emotionally safe to declare to their peers that they are materially wealthy. They can grow up with that central question in the back of their minds. If people know about the wealth in my family, will they like me or love me for who I am or for the money and wealth—the valuables I have access to? Will other people be honest with me or will they always have an ulterior agenda because I am wealthy?

Some rich kids do grow up with a sense of resentment over coming from a wealthy family. Rich kids can also be ambivalent and confused about being wealthy. On one hand there is this resentment over the wealth, and yet the same wealth brings creature comforts, ease, power, and status.

"Being wealthy makes me feel detached and separate from my peers." says Natalie, a third-generation member of a business-owning family. Natalie shared with me that she wants to be a part of her peer group, yet her fear of being seen as one of those rich spoiled brats holds her back from being herself, and she lies about what she can and cannot afford.

"I hate my parents for this, because I feel I can't be myself with people who are outside my family circle and who do not have the same amount of money or wealth as we do."

In working with Natalie, we identified her Money Motto,™ a belief or feeling one has about money and wealth, as "Money makes me feel like a hypocrite." Natalie's Money Motto™ comes from a lifetime of seeing her parents behave a certain way with their similarly wealthy peers, and yet they behave in a completely different way with people of lower socio-economic means. Given the significant influence parental behavior has on the upbringing of children, Natalie's parents' double-standard way of behaving around people of lower socio-economic means greatly contributed to Natalie's Money Motto.™ Her beliefs and feelings about money created a great rift between Natalie and her parents, especially her father. When Natalie and I first started working together, one of her stated desires was to find a way to reconnect with her father, whom she loved dearly, but from whom as a late teen, she had experienced a growing distance, for which she had no clear explanation. Through our coaching sessions, and once we uncovered her Money Motto™ of "Money makes me feel like a hypocrite," Natalie was able achieve some clarity over her associations of wealth and money with the distant relationship she had with her father—since he was the economic engine providing the money and wealth for the family. Her feelings of shame and fear of being seen as a "rich, spoiled brat" by her peers, led to her to being angry with her father who she blamed for her own apparent lack of ability to be an open and honest member of her peer group. Natalie realized her anger towards her father was because she felt he was to blame for her difficulties in connecting with her peers; his fault because he was wealthy and, as a result, so was she.

Through some further coaching sessions, Natalie was able to create a new Money Motto.™ "Money allows me to be myself," one that serves her much more successfully, and allows her to be more fully, genuinely self-expressive, which included being more comfortable about being wealthy and no longer being ashamed of her family's wealth. Sounds too simple? Well, really, it isn't all that difficult, given appropriate support. Once Natalie was able to embrace and be comfortable with who she is, all of who she is—this includes being from a wealthy family—she was able to be more open and self-disclosing around her peers. The other benefit arising for Natalie, as a result of redefining her Money Motto™ was that she was able to reconnect with her father. They have a much closer relationship with each other than ever she thought possible. They have also developed a common language, and can openly have conversations about each other's Money Motto™ and the impact their respective mottos have on each other as well as on all of their other relationships.

Unlike Natalie and her father, most children and their parents don't realize what has happened to them until they are much older. Not needing to work in order to live is one of the toughest challenges young wealthy inheritors have to face. It is a predicament that can lead to low self-esteem, and erode confidence. One of the strongest needs of the human spirit is to have a sense of purpose in one's life and to know that you are making a meaningful contribution to something that is motivated by more than self-interest. Meaningful work provides a sense of purpose as well as a contribution to the collective—family, community, society, or nation. In some cases, children of wealth resent it having only learned to be dependent on their family's wealth. Never having to save for something—deferring gratification— is another challenge since it can lead to an inordinate sense of entitlement, impatience, and a lack of social responsibility.

Don't just give your children valuables (money is a Great White Elephant™). Instead, equip them with values and prepare them emotionally to ensure the gift of money and wealth is not destined to be nothing other than a burden foisted upon them. Teach them to be comfortable with being wealthy and educate them about the responsibility that comes with having material wealth. Model a sensible work ethic for them. Teach and share with them your wisdom and what you have learned along the way. Just because your children are now adults does not mean that their childhood desires of wanting to spend time with dad or mom have diminished. Such genuine desires might be buried under some emotional baggage or conflicted feelings towards a parent, but once that baggage is unpacked and conflicted feelings are resolved, they will want to make up for lost time, just like you did. Just like Natalie and her father.

Questions to Ponder...

1. What is your "why"?

2. What is your Great White Elephant™ as it relates to your "why"?

3. Are your valuables aligned with your "why"?

4. What are you projecting onto your children?

5. What can you do to develop a closer loving relationship with your children?

3

A TALE OF PERSPECTIVES

We judge others by their behavior.
We judge ourselves by our intentions.
— IAN PERCY —

What Color Are Your Spectacles and Are You Even Listening?

To forgive is to set a prisoner free and discover that the prisoner was you.
— LEWIS B. SMEDES —

I AM PARTICIPATING IN A LANDMARK FORUM and the forum leader, Anika, is at the front of the room addressing the audience. Anika is Dutch and has an aura about her that I would describe as one of arrogance. I quickly found myself not liking her and realized there was something about her demeanor that I found offensive. I did not particularly like her accent and, while I was conscious that I had made this mean something more than it should—I wasn't sure what—I just knew I didn't like her accent.

I had made an effort to find what I felt was a strategically placed seat in the second row from the front and next to an aisle. This way I had given myself room to stretch my legs and only had to accommodate another person next to me on one side—a position which meant I could only reasonably be expected to speak with one stranger. I recall feeling a bit anxious and nervous, being unsure of what the weekend would hold or reveal. These feelings were not new for me. I had experienced similar reservations many times, like being in the company of an acquaintance with whom I don't feel entirely at ease. These feelings usually manifest themselves as a knot in my stomach and a general feeling of bodily tension. Outwardly, I know I appear to others as confident and perhaps even that I have it all together. Not true!

Anika is busy explaining the schedule for the weekend and what we—the participants—can expect. As she is talking, I am sitting with my thoughts and feelings, and looking around the room to try and get some sort of handle on who is in the room with me—what kind of people are here and maybe learn why they have chosen to attend. At some point, after what felt like an eternity to me—because I was being impatient and wanted to get the show on the road—the forum leader asked us if we had any questions. I don't recall exactly what any of the other participants asked, but I do recall feeling frustrated as I found myself judging one person after another for asking what I thought were useless and irrelevant questions. Anika answered all of the questions with grace and ease.

Anika then proceeded to inform all of us that we had not been listening to her and had not really been present in the room with her for the past hour and a half. I felt wronged by her comments and, quite frankly, judged by her, and found myself liking her even less. I regarded her point of view as arrogant and self-righteous and her projection of superiority one to be despised. In hindsight, I understand how I had already seen and heard her from the outset from a place of dismissal and disdain. I had made up my mind about who she was without ever really knowing her. In essence, I had judged her and had determined that I would only see her in a particularly negative light.

Anika tells us that we have not really been listening. What we have been doing instead is assessing, judging, making decisions, criticizing, and blaming. Furthermore, we have not really been present in the room. Instead, we have been with our thoughts and feelings, doing all of the things she said we have been doing— assessing, judging, making decisions, criticizing, and blaming.

Anika then tells us about what distinguishes a Landmark Forum from many others of similar ilk. It is what they refer to as "already always listening." As human beings, most of us, most of the time, have a way of listening to others; it is a way of listening that we are not really fully aware of. This way of listening is based on our perceptions of others and how we see them or how they present themselves to us.

Whenever I make a presentation to a group, I usually ask for a volunteer to demonstrate this concept of "already always listening." I ask the volunteer to take their time in looking around the room, noting who is wearing blue—or a shade of it—make a tally of those people and keep the number to themselves. I then ask the same volunteer to close their eyes and tell us how many people in the room are wearing a shade of red. Nine times out of ten, they cannot give me an accurate number.

How is this possible? They began by carefully looking around the room as per the instructions I had given. When asked why they cannot recall how many people are wearing some shade of red, most volunteers eventually answer that since they were not asked to take note of those wearing any shade of red, they didn't pay attention to or count those who were. This is what happens in relationships. We focus on seeing only some aspects of another person—only a part of who they really are. As a result of what we choose to pay attention to, we make decisions and judgments about them, and thereafter listen to them and treat them according to the narrow perspective we have formed. We then look for additional evidence to reinforce our narrow perspective of them and this only further validates—in our own mind—what we choose to listen out for and how we hear them. It is this sort of prematurely formed perspective and narrow view of others that many times prevents us from having rich and rewarding relationships with others and which potentially robs us of ever truly getting to know someone. Instead we find ourselves judging and dismissing others all because we have this perspective and are "already always listening" to them.

I am standing in front of the microphone, at the front of the room. Anika asks me why I came and what it is I hope to learn from attending a Landmark Forum. I say I am here to forgive my mother. Anika says, "so do it; make the decision and forgive her right now." In that moment, the realization hits me that I have held on to a limited perspective of my mother for more than twenty years. For all this time, I have been seeing my mother as weak, needy, and clingy. I have also been hearing her from that same perspective. I would hear those things in the tone of her voice, in the words she would use to communicate with me, in the questions she would ask. Standing in front of the participants at the Landmark Forum, I found myself become completely aware of the narrow and unflattering perspective I had long held about my mother. In the face of the realization, I knew I could no longer avoid admitting and acknowledging it. It had to be dealt with. For a long time, I had not had any sort of meaningful relationship with my mother. I could not stand being with her for more than a few minutes at a time. Being an only child from an Italian family, I had a truckload of conflict within me arising out of what I felt for my mother. I felt I had an obligation to love her and should have a genuine desire to spent time with her. Given that she is now seventy years old—and who knows how much time she has left—I knew it was becoming increasingly important to find a way to spend more time with her, and do that in a harmonious frame of mind. I decided there and then to forgive my mother. I forgive her for her own way of being and forgive myself at the same time for how harshly I had judged her and blamed her for how her way of being affected me and the way I treated her in response. A feeling of lightness came over me. I felt as if a great weight had been lifted from me. Anika then asked me when I was going to call my mother and share with her what I had just experienced and learned.

During the next break in the session, I made the decision to call my mother and share with her the insight I had gained and take responsibility for my role in the lack of communication between us. I dialed her number and the first thing I noticed was that I was neither anxious nor dreading the call. I actually felt pleasantly surprised over how excited I was to be about to talk to my mom. The phone rang a couple of times and my mother eventually answered:

"Hello."

"Hi mom, how are you?"

"Okay." (In the past I would have heard her response as weak and clingy.)

"I am attending a seminar and I have experienced something I would like to share with you. For the longest time, I experienced you as being weak, needy, and clingy and as a result of this new perspective I have been judging you and withholding my love and not wanting to spend time with you. I am responsible for how I have behaved because of these judgments and I am deeply sorry for having withheld my love. What I want to create with you is a loving relationship, one where I want to be with you and enjoy your company as I try to get to know you again."

After a long silence on the other end of the phone, my mom says: "My prayers have been answered, I finally have my son back."

Today I enjoy spending time with my mother and sharing my life with her. She has become one of my most trusted advisors.

Who Are You Being as a Leader in Your Life?

The mastery of the art of Leadership comes with the mastery of the self,
and so developing leadership is a process of developing the self.
— KOUZES & POSNER in *A Leader's Legacy* —

It is easy to look at those with whom we are in relationship, see all of their faults and point the finger at them. We can also make them a convenient scapegoat for all of our own difficulties, shortcomings, and problematic circumstances. Sometimes, all we want to see is their issues and focus on how we think and feel they behave towards us.

Looking inside yourself requires courage and integrity. To monitor our own behavior and be accountable for our own role in a relationship can be both frightening as well as liberating. Being able to "see" a relationship—perhaps for the first time—for what it really is can be a tipping point. Examining how we enter into relationship with others and when we are in relationship, how we tend to conduct ourselves with others, are critical steps towards achieving some greater clarity over our own emotional and psychological evolution (maturity) and will always help us determine where we are at and where we may want or need to go in any particular relationship.

It is important that this self-examination of how we behave in relationships starts with the most important relationship of all—the relationship we have with ourselves. After all, if we want to be in healthy and meaningful relationships with others, it makes sense—at least to me—to examine the relationship we have with ourselves. There may be no better place to begin exploring the relationship we have with ourselves than to look for our own Great White Elephants.

It is important to emphasis that there is not one single Great White Elephant™ in our lives; there are many and they show up in a multitude of ways. They do not have to be great things or big issues that are not dealt with. Great White Elephants can be small, subtle things, like missing conversations either with ourselves and/or with others, perceptions of ourselves/or others, negative thoughts we have of others/or ourselves, and our limiting beliefs that, if not addressed or dealt with in an appropriate and timely fashion, have the potential to become massive issues.

Over the past five or six months, since first I developed the idea for this book, a significant part of my waking life has been focused on drafting an outline, writing and more writing, after some structural and substantive editing. As I get to a point in the process where I can see light at the end of the tunnel, I would like to share that I've also experienced considerable upheaval and something of a transformation in my life too.

Just to let you know, I didn't write the chapters of this book in linear fashion, beginning to end. My style is more free-flowing, and stream of consciousness-driven, by which I mean my writing is colored by what is going on in the moment for me, and influenced by my feelings and emotions as much as my thoughts and ideas.

When I say my life has been transformed, as I look at myself today, I see a different man than the one I saw last year. I have acknowledged, embraced, and released my feelings of fear, and not feeling safe. I now see how those thoughts and feelings were keeping me from being my authentic self. I now see how not feeling safe was holding me back from being the leader in my life, not just a leader in my chosen profession, but also a leader as a father, friend, and intimate partner. Not feeling safe was taking away my power and potential as a leader.

This chapter was written this past February, while I was presenting at a conference at the Japer Park Lodge, Alberta. I had some down time and took advantage of the inspiration of the mountain environment to reflect upon the relationship I have with myself. I found myself being more comfortable with my own company. I discovered that I have a stronger, clearer, more direct connection with myself than I can ever remember having experienced in the past. I have become really clear about my own Great White Elephants. In journaling about what has changed,

I am aware that I have embraced all of who I am—the good, the bad, and the ugly. With this I have a greater sense of acceptance of who I am, warts and all. I now see how self-acceptance is the first step towards self-love.

What does any of this mean, the adult in me asks? Why am I including an account of this most personal journey in this book? I know some of you readers will be asking yourself a similar question: What has any of this got to do with business succession planning and the transition of wealth?

Well, my answer for you is everything! It has everything to do with how you approach your business succession planning and the transitioning of your wealth.

Succession planning and the transfer of your wealth to the next generation requires and demands you step up to be an authentic leader for yourself and your family. In the transition process it is important to know what you are transitioning, it's not just your valuables and your values. You have to get clear about the Great White Elephants you carry with respect to your beliefs and behaviors as they relate to ownership, power, and money. Leadership is about clarity. Authentic leadership is about walking your talk, congruency of self. But before you do that you must be clear on your talk, especially one's self talk. Once one is congruent, you can have conversations that clean up the past, and establish new commitments for your relationships. Before this can happen, you must be connected to self and your authentic leader.

In the past, I could not have either talked or written about what connection really was or what it meant to me. The type of connection I am talking about is being clear, and ultimately being congruent with who I say I am and how I choose to be, based on who I say I am. I did not always fully understand what it really meant any more than I understood the depth of the power associated with it. Six months ago, I would have described the connection as something out there as opposed to the connection I have with or within myself. Only when we are truly connected with ourselves and our inner, authentic leader, can we find our power; our ability to operate with integrity, honesty, and transparency. The power to be ourselves, and not have to worry or be concerned about what others may think about us.

What I didn't see or fully grasp before this time was the need for a deeper connection with myself. How can I possibly be connected with others, if I am not connected with myself and who I really am when I enter into relationship with others? I am now much more aware of the connection I have with myself. As a result of a deeper connection with myself, I am more accepting of myself and am learning to be more loving of myself as well.

What does this deeper connection with self look and feel like? Well, I am much more aware of my thoughts in the moment, which have an influence on how I feel, which in turn determines who I am being and how I am behaving in the moment.

- Thoughts
- Feelings
- Being

As human beings we have myriad thoughts every day. We are not aware of most of these thoughts, and they are really the equivalent of the background music you are sometimes aware of in an elevator: musak! Most times you walk into an elevator, you might be aware of hearing music; most times you are oblivious to it, even though it is playing in the background. Why is this the case? Well, mostly, it's because we are having a conversation with someone else or that we are preoccupied with our own thoughts; typically whatever is front-of-mind. What is usually front-of-mind is whatever it is—some task we are about to undertake or whatever it is we are about to deal with; it could also be some pressing personal issue over which we have some worry, anxiety, or concern. Whatever it is—whether it is the next task or some pressing concern—these are the thoughts we are most conscious of and all of our other thoughts fade into the background, just like the musak in the elevator.

Despite the fact we remain unaware of most of our thoughts, they continue to exert a significant influence over the way in which we live our lives and thus we live out of a place where our largely unconscious thoughts dictate our being in the world. In essence, what we spend time thinking about, we manifest or bring about in the world. What we think about elicits feelings, and our feelings will largely dictate the way we behave, conduct, or present ourselves. Sometimes, our way of being in the world is disconnected from our most authentic selves. That is, our present way of being may not be truly representative of who we really are.

Over these past six months I have worked hard to reconnect with my authentic self. What does this really mean? One of the aspects of myself with which I had become disconnected was the ability to have compassion for myself. I find I can muster vast amounts of compassion for others, yet when I need to be compassionate with myself, there is nothing left. Here's how this imbalance has played out in my life. As I have previously mentioned, a relationship with a woman whom I loved dearly and deeply ended recently. The breakup caused me emotional pain to an extent that I have never before experienced. Numerous times over the past weeks and months, I have found myself in a dark place of sadness, regret, hurt, and loneliness. The emotional pain was, at times, unbearable to a point where ending my life became a serious consideration. I've spent many nights alone in my house, sitting in the dark and drinking far too much, just wanting the pain to go away, because I found it almost impossible to just be with the pain. There are two good reasons why I did not act rashly and do something stupid: my two children and the love I have for the work I do with my clients in my private practice.

In allowing myself to feel all of my feelings, I have realized my need to treat myself with compassion for all that I have been through with the demise of this relationship. I realize now, that I cannot force my way out of the situation I am in; I cannot fake my way out of it; I must feel my way out of it. I must be gentle with myself and have abundant compassion for this man, who is hurting deeply and missing his intimate partner. Just as I felt great love for my intimate partner, I must be prepared to endure similarly powerful feelings over the demise of the relationship.

Another realization has been that I have been collapsing suffering into feeling. I have always had it in mind that they are one and the same—that suffering is the same thing as a feeling. They are not. As a friend of mine said to me: "Suffering is optional, feeling is mandatory." It is imperative that I acknowledge all my feelings, as this will allow me to eventually get through them. However, I realize now, I don't have to suffer, all I have to do is feel. I also do not have to judge myself too harshly for what and how I feel or for how long the grieving process takes.

I share this recent personal history with you, so that you might ask yourself what is it in or about your own life that you can't sit with, particularly as it relates to your relationship with ownership, power, and money and as a part of the business succession planning and wealth transfer process you might be going through at this time. You could also think about these same issues—what is it that isn't sitting well with you at this time—that is interfering or undermining your ability to bring your most authentic self to the world? In my own example, I could not be with compassion and gentleness for myself. In the context of this book, a lack of compassion and gentleness towards myself were one of my Great White Elephants. Thus, if we are not aware of our thoughts and related feelings that arise from those thoughts, then our lack of awareness or ignorance has the potential to become a Great White Elephant™ that undermines our future actions and plans.

Whatever it is that you cannot be with as it relates to ownership, power, or money and with respect to your business succession planning and intentions for the transference of wealth will become an undercurrent and invade the headspace of your planning. It will interfere with and undermine the process. What you cannot be with or sit with, to use my example of not being able to have compassion for myself, was interfering with and in the way of my healing from a broken heart. Who you are not being, or what you can not be with, whatever that is as it relates to ownership, power, and money is a Great White Elephant™ in your business succession planning and intentions for the transference of wealth.

What Is It that You Cannot Be With?

We don't see things as they are; we see things as we are.
— ANAIS NIN —

This might be a bit of a strange question to ask, but do you recall that I earlier shared that I could not be with my mother's neediness or, perhaps more accurately and honestly, I could not be with my perception of her being needy. Typically what one cannot be with in another person is a reflection of our own issues, and we are rejecting this truth and projecting onto another person. In the case of my mother, I could not be with her neediness because I have a hard time being with my own neediness in intimate relationships. So, I wronged my mother and was hard on myself all out of avoiding dealing with my own needs. In order to be with my own neediness as well as own my perceptions of my mother's neediness, I have to embrace my own neediness, and I can only do that when I stop considering it as wrong or weak of me to have legitimate needs. It is only in embracing what we have either rejected about ourselves, or projected onto others, that we can really be with what we don't want to be with.

Here's an example of how this all works and plays out in familial relationships. In working with Betsy, a member of the second generation of a client family, we were able to identify what Betsy could not be with in her relationship with a nephew, Gregory. Betsy had always held the view that Gregory had an inordinate sense of entitlement—as if money grew on trees. Presently, Gregory does not work in the family business, but is a shareholder and receives a healthy income from dividends that funds his lifestyle.

In coaching Betsy, she shared how she felt guilty for never having to work throughout her life and being in receipt of dividends from the family business for as long as she can remember. Her

Money Motto™ of "Money allows me to fit in and gives me access to people of similar financial standing," has been a challenge for Betsy, because she has never really felt that she fit into the family business. As a result of these beliefs, Betsy has never felt that she deserved money or wealth. Because she does not work in the family business, Betsy feels she is not contributing or adding value to the business. Yet, at her core, she has a strong sense of entitlement arising from her family name and what it means to be a socialite.

When I pointed out that Betsy was projecting her sense of entitlement and guilt over not contributing to the family business that funds her lifestyle onto her nephew Gregory, she realized why she has never been able to develop a meaningful relationship with her nephew, her brother's only son. As a result of coaching and working with us, Betsy was able to repair her relationship with her nephew, and admit to him the real reasons for her disdain and distant relationship.

Betsy was able to share her Great White Elephant™ that she characterized as her own sense of entitlement and guilt over not feeling like she made a meaningful contribution to the family business. Betsy became authentic about her inauthenticity with her nephew. The conversation was a turning point in the relationship between aunt and nephew. Betsy owned up to her feelings for what she had been projecting onto Gregory, took responsibility for the impact of her actions in her relationship with Gregory, and made a new commitment to develop a different kind of relationship with Gregory—one characterized by openness, transparency, compassion, and mutual respect.

This was all possible because Betsy was able to create a new relationship with herself, one that was based on openness, transparency, compassion, and respect for herself. One of the contributing factors for Betsy to be with herself in this new way was to create a new Money Motto,™ one that served her and the family more harmoniously which she defined as: "My value is my commitment to fitting in." We were able to assist Betsy in creating a new Money Motto,™ out of which Betsy was able to reinforce a more positive self-image. In undertaking this work on herself, Betsy was able to more easily manifest what she has always wanted and desired, which is to feel valued and make a more significant contribution to her family business. Betsy's role is to lead the activities of the family foundation and have controlling authority over the deployment of funds from the foundation. As Betsy has become more comfortable in handling and dealing with money and wealth, she has also become more accomplished and successful in raising money for the foundation.

From Princess to Queen

If you are being run out of town,
get in front of the crowd and make it look like a parade.
— UNKNOWN —

Elizabeth, or Auntie Lizzy, has she is affectionately called by her nieces and nephews, is the matriarch of a large, successful and influential family. Lizzy is the second oldest child of four and the only daughter. She started working in the family business— just like all of her brothers—in the front office. Lizzy's father always told Lizzy, just like the others, you own a quarter of this business. However, what Lizzy had always been told and what actually occurred were not congruent. Even though Lizzy worked in the family business she was rarely included in any discussion regarding plans for its future direction or its financial affairs.

Lizzy has always felt that she is not safe to express herself and as a result has basically shut down. This self-imposed silence is largely due to the manner in which Lizzy has been treated as the only daughter.

When we started working together, Lizzy got present to her Great White Elephant,™ which she described as still being angry over the way she has been treated, first by her father and later by her brothers.

This Great White Elephant™ has kept Lizzy feeling apart from the rest of the family, a feeling compounded by the belief that she has felt discarded by the men in her life. Lizzy feels she has been given a figurehead title and a role as the chairperson of the Family Office.

Lizzy wants to create a legacy wherein the women of the family are seen and treated as equals. This is something that she feels is sorely missing in her family.

Out of our work together, Lizzy has committed to becoming the champion for the women in her family; this so that they can be seen as equals, be empowered, respected, valued, and included; all of the things that Lizzy so desperately wanted and sought from her father and brothers. The process of letting go of the anger and resentment, along with her inability to forgive herself, was difficult at the outset because Lizzy was not able to identify with or fully manifest a new self while hanging onto these habitual thoughts.

If Lizzy was to become the Queen and champion for the other women in her family, as she had committed to doing, she would also have to be willing to work through a metaphorical wardrobe change with respect to her thoughts, feelings, and way of being in her family.

At first Lizzy fought this, because her identity with the angry, resentful, unforgiving princess was so entrenched. I had to show Lizzy the payoff-penalties associated with her hanging onto these feelings and way of being. The payoff-penalties Lizzy was able to distinguish for herself included:

- Lizzy gets to remain the victim.
- Lizzy does not have to take the responsibility for becoming the champion for the other women in the family.
- Lizzy does not have acknowledge her fear of her own power; hence she pushes it away and avoids it.
- Lizzy gets to be right.
- Lizzy gets to stay small and avoids stepping into her legitimate role of becoming the Queen of the family.

Once Lizzy got to see the payoffs, she decided that the legacy she wanted to create was far too important to relinquish in spite of her personal and emotional constraints.

So, what is Lizzy up to today? She is starting to step into the role of Queen for the family, and champion of the women. She has forgiven herself, her father, and her brothers. As a result she now know she contributes to the family business through the Family Office, by having created a sense of togetherness and inclusion with her brothers. This has been something of an example to the next generation about what is possible when one person and ultimately a whole generation faces up to and deals with their own individual and collective Great White Elephants.

Today, the members of this family are experiencing a sense of full self-expression, respect for each other, as well as an enhanced feeling of personal safety and interconnection. All of this is due to the fact that Aunt Lizzy had the courage to face her Great White

Elephants and change how she felt, and recreate her way of being, by changing her perspective.

Questions to Ponder...

1. What have you still not forgiven yourself for?

2. Who do you need to forgive?

3. Who are you being as the leader of your own life?

4. What emotion can you not be with?

5. What family member can you not be with?

6. What is the extent of your accountability for whatever and to whomever you cannot be with?

4

THE MONEY MOTTO™

When you let money speak for you,
it drowns out anything else you meant to say.
— MIGNON McLAUGHLIN, *The Second Neurotic's Notebook* —

Who is Really Running your Life?

Clarity of vision depends on knowing what is really important.
— JIM CLEMMER —

LET'S CONSIDER MONEY IN THE CONTEXT OF IT BEING or becoming a Great White Elephant.™ Money is obviously valuable, and yet it can become a significant burden if given too frequently and too early on in life. Yet the way we usually think and talk about money in a social context, is from an entirely quantitative perspective. How much we make, how much we spend, how our accountant reduced our taxes, and how much we have saved for retirement. We give little or no thought to how we feel about money. Since we are human beings, who have feelings, and we have feelings about people, places, experiences, and material possessions, we also have feelings about money; our feelings about money, however well we might understand them or think we understand them, lead to a way of behaving with money, and how we deal with it in all aspects of our life. Our way of dealing with money has the potential for becoming a Great White Elephant™ for us or for our family. Not knowing one's Money Motto™ and its impact is one serious money-related Great White Elephant.™

We all have a way of being with money. Some of us are responsible with money, and some of us are not. Regardless of how we behave with money, we all have a relationship with it. I suggest money is just another reflection of who you are at your core. For my first book, *Life After Wealth:® When is Enough Enough?* I conducted a little research because I was curious to see if there was any sort of correlation between how we treat our money and how we treat those closest to us, including ourselves. What I discovered was very interesting, yet not particularly surprising in hindsight. How we treat our money turned out to be an accurate reflection of how we treat ourselves as well as others, especially those with whom we are close—the ones we say we love.

For example, if one is the kind of individual who gives freely of themselves in terms of time, attention, energy, and love, then the chances are high that they share or give away their money with a similar freedom. One might call these people generous. This is usually all okay, so as long as they are not giving away too much of themselves. People would consider me to be most generous, with my time, love for others and with my money. But under the table, my Great White Elephant™ is that I feel and believe I am not particularly valued or valuable, and so I try to buy or justify my value by being generous, by giving away too much, sometime to an extent that is to my own detriment.

Another example would be the kind of individual that does not believe they deserve money and wealth. In such a person as this, their tendency might be to invest in things that blow up, just to prove to their sub-conscious that they don't deserve the money. If one looks closely, you might see that this kind of person will have a similar tendency to treat relationships in like fashion. Once things are going well in a relationship, they will do or say something potentially destructive that undermines or sabotages the future of the relationship.

Since we all have a relationship with our money, and we are relationship-oriented beings, we take our relationship with money into all of our other significant relationships. Beginning with the relationship we have with ourselves, and moving outwards to those intimate relationships with our spouse or life partner, to the other members of our family, to those at work and in our business activities—our colleagues and co-workers, to our friends and acquaintances, and throughout our various communities of interaction, including our voluntary and charitable works, even into our succession and wealth transition plans. Does it not make sense to uncover and understand the true nature of our relationship with money and the impact it has on all of these other relationships?

All of us have scripts we play in our head and, for better or worse, these scripts affect our lives in ways that are more significant than most of us would care to admit. Many of us live each day listening to scripts such as: "I'm too fat," or "I'm too thin," or "I'm too dumb." For many of us, we recite such messages as these to ourselves all too frequently, and the outcome is that we no long recognize what we are doing. Unfortunately, these scripts are usually more negative than positive in their impact and, without realizing it, many of us have allowed the scripts to dictate our behavior—to the extent that they exert a powerful influence over the way we live our lives.

Just as we have scripts about ourselves, we have scripts about money. Although we may have a variety of scripts about money, we usually have one that stands out as a central belief. I call this script our Money Motto.™ The following are examples of commonly held Money Motto's:™

- More money means more control
- Money allows me to fit in
- Money makes me lovable
- Money is a measure of my worth

Determining the origin of our primary Money Motto™ can be a complex and challenging process, because our subconscious beliefs about money evolve and are likely a composite derived from both our childhood as well as more recent adult life experiences. Your Money Motto™ can either be an empowering or destructive influence, regardless of your conscious awareness of its existence. If we are conscious of our Money Motto,™ and it is basically an empowering one to have, we still may not know how to exploit it constructively and to maximum positive effect. Similarly, if we are consciously aware of our Money Motto,™ and it is unhealthy and potentially destructive, we may need support and assistance in creating a new and more positive Money Motto.™

My experience has led me to believe that most people are not consciously aware of their Money Motto.™ If we cannot name our Money Motto,™ nor recognize whether its influence is empowering or destructive, or even if it has any validity, then we run the risk of allowing it to motivate or dictate our behavior and the relationship we have with money and wealth. If we remain unconscious of our Money Motto™ then it will continue to operate in ways that are not necessarily congruent with our values or in alignment with what matters most—our goals and dreams. It is our beliefs about money and wealth which dictate our financial decisions—from how we earn our money, to how we spend it, negotiate for it, invest it, transition it, inherit it, and gift it. In order to achieve clarity around our current beliefs about money, it is helpful to make our best effort and return to our earliest awareness of money. For most of us, this occurred within the family home, with our family of origin.

The Kitchen Table:
Our Introduction to the Money Motto™

What counts is what you do with your money,

not where it came from.

— MERTON MILLER —

Have you ever taken the time to reflect on when and where you first learned about money? Whenever I ask my clients this question, nearly everyone provides the same or a very similar answer: the kitchen table—the very first family boardroom! Within most homes, the kitchen table is the place where children have the opportunity to hear discussions about family and work or business issues. In most cases, such discussions include the subject of money. Some of you might be thinking "But money wasn't discussed in my home." The absence of any discussion about money is as significant as any discussion about money that did take place. Not talking about money is also a way of communicating about money. Some families have a Great White Elephant™ regarding money. They know they have to have the conversation, yet they don't know how. Whether or not you recall your parents having conversations about finances, money and wealth, children receive messages and develop thoughts and feelings on the matter.

Many parents don't know how to initiate a conversation about money and wealth. Like most of us, they probably assume that it has to start with the quantitative side of things, the numbers and possessions, the disclosing of a will and trust documents. These matters can be daunting and complicated topics as well as intimidating and uncomfortable because they underscore, in so many ways, the transient nature of time and a human life; one day, the older generation is going to die and what are we supposed to do with anything they leave for us to inherit? In addition many parents feel that if they disclose the "numbers" to their children this could have some sort of detrimental effect upon them. Children are not as uninformed as many parents might think. If a family is wealthy, then the children will have some awareness of the extent of that wealth, simply because they can observe the quality of lifestyle their parents lead and provide for them. Just look at your home, the cars you drive, where you take vacations, and for some among you, the private jet and number of staff you employ to support your private lifestyle. If some of you are thinking your children have no awareness of the extent of your wealth, think again.

A conversation about money and wealth is not necessarily about simply disclosing the numbers. It's about having the conversations that reveal how you, as their parents, feel about money (i.e., your own Money Motto™); conversations that clarify your core values and through which you can declare what matters most. Likewise, ask your children how they might feel about money. It is important for your children to know with clarity what your intentions are, and what these intentions are based on. We get back to the reasons "why." Once a child knows and understands the "why," they are in a much better position to understand the decisions you have made with regard to your money and as well as the impact these decisions will have on their future lives. Just as important as any of this, a parent might want to consider learning each child's Money Motto,™ their personal values, and their own dreams and desires for the future.

It is difficult to articulate and share something like a Money Motto,™ when one does not know what their Money Motto™ is or where it came from. Take a moment to consider how money was dealt with in your home when you were a child. Was it ever discussed, and what was the energy and tone behind those conversations. What were your parent's beliefs about money and what sort of behavior did they exhibit around it—both in handling it and talking about it?

As I moved through my journey to authenticity, by uncovering my own Great White Elephants about money, I was compelled to ask myself these questions in order to get to the root origin of my own beliefs about money. Although it was, at times, a difficult process, I took myself back in time to reflect on how money was dealt with (or not dealt with) in my home as a child.

High Society Façade

Mirrors should think longer before they reflect.
— JEAN COCTEAU —

My mother was born in Chile in the thirties, when the military were in power, and she was adopted into an important military family (a brigadier general's family to be exact). I recall my mother sharing a story with me about the day when, as a young girl, she was sent off to boarding school. While away, my mother's stepparents would send her dolls to keep her company at the school. Sadly, my mother felt that she did not fit in, and as a result of her loneliness, she would give the dolls away in an attempt to foster friendships with the other girls.

My mother's life of privilege continued when she married my father, who frequently showered her with expensive gifts. It is out of these experiences, I believe, that my mother developed a sense of superiority and entitlement, and with all of the material gifts she received, believed herself to be wealthy. Life circumstances changed drastically for my mother after my father died. Today she lives in a small apartment and has little or no net worth. Regardless, she continues to behave like a wealthy dowager, wearing fur coats and often treats people in the service industry with disdain.

Based on my mother's behavior throughout my life and the stories she told me of her youth, I inherited the message that money was a means by which you could fit in; it could make you feel important, and it was how one made friends and gained respect.

Money is How I Show I Love You

You give but little when you give of your possessions.
It is when you give of yourself that you truly give.
— KAHLIL GIBRAN, *The Prophet* —

My father was born in Sicily in the twenties and, like many European men of his era, he never learned how to directly express his feelings. Looking back, I cannot recall a single instance when my father told me he loved me, or that he was proud of me, or that I was special. I remember craving his approval and affection as a child. I played a great deal of rugby growing up, and I can clearly resurrect the hopeful feelings I had but kept locked inside come game time, as I looked with the hope of seeing my father among the spectators. He never did come to watch me play rugby.

I was asked once how I had experienced my father as a child. My response at the time was that I had experienced my father as a piece of furniture; he was just there. What my father lacked in emotional intimacy, he tried to make up for with money. My father showed his affection by buying his family material possessions. When my father returned from his latest international business trip, he would express his affection towards my mother with another piece of jewelry. As unable as he was in creating any emotional intimacy with my mother, so it was between my father and me. I recall one Christmas in particular when I woke up to something like thirty or forty Christmas presents under the tree. However, when my father died, he left my mother with no life insurance and no investments. What he did leave her with was a mortgage and the collection of jewelry he had purchased for her over the years. Since my father had not known how to show his emotions, he had compensated for this by buying us material possessions. Looking back, all I really wanted was a father who was present, not always and only one who brought me presents.

Money Allows Me to Fit In

Men make counterfeit money;
in many more cases, money makes counterfeit men.
— SYDNEY J. HARRIS —

By the time I was 29 I had been working in the wealth management industry for 5 years, and was making what I thought (at the time) was a lot of money. I was behaving from a place of ego, trying desperately to portray the image that I was a "big shot" with lots of cash. I took great pains to ensure that my outward appearance suggested I was successful and happy; however, on the inside my spirit was dying. What I did not realize was that my life and behavior were motivated by the belief that "money allows me to fit in." I had been living with this destructive Money Motto™ for most of my life, but I was completely unaware of how its impact was showing up in my life, my relationship with my spouse (at that time), my family, my friends, and my business.

My life was out of control, and I was doing everything I could to maintain my carefully constructed façade.

In examining my own life and past behavior, I can definitely see a parallel between the way I treated others (and myself) and the way I treated my money.

I began by examining my own life according to this hypothesis. I grew up in a home where money was used as a way to convey and confirm status (intrinsically it fostered a false sense of security and superiority and extrinsically it supported the illusion of social status that comes with apparent material wealth) and as a means of showing affection. This foundation, in combination with my early experiences of rejection and bullying, led me to the conclusion that if I made a lot of money, I could "buy my way" into being accepted and having friends. As a result, I was continually spending my money to uphold an image of success in an attempt to gain friends. I had submerged myself so deeply in this façade that I had no idea how to find my way out. I didn't take the time to be authentic and to connect on an intimate level with others or myself. Focusing on money was a way for me to hide from the world, a way to try and prevent and certainly avoid the pain of rejection. At the time, I had yet to realize that no amount of money could buy me the feeling of belonging I needed most—self-acceptance. At the time, I did not value myself, and, consequently, I could not value the money I was acquiring.

A decade later, after some considerable further work on my journey of personal growth—I can truly say I value myself, and my money. It was a journey that required me to first address the negative beliefs and behaviors that were present in my life. I achieved this through working to identify and understand my Money Motto.™

When I think of my own parents, it is easy to understand how their Money Motto™ affected their behavior. My father's Money Motto™ would likely have been something close to: "Money is how I show you that I love you," and my mother's would be: "Money makes me important." For myself, the Money Motto™ I lived with for most of my life was: "Money allows me to fit in." Unfortunately, it took the dissolution of my first marriage, the loss of most of my net worth, and my own soul/sanity, before I realized:

1. I had a Money Motto,™ and
2. It wasn't working for me!

A Father's Legacy

What we do, is what we are committed to.
— KEVIN BROWN —

Stephen grew up in a small town in the US Midwest and lived there until he was about 12 years old. His family then relocated to a major metropolitan city where his father bought a five and dime store. Money was never discussed at their dinner table and a subject the family spent little time thinking about. The family was always comfortable, very middle class and there were never any worries about money. After high school, Stephen went to college and his parents were able to pay for his studies. Stephen never considered his family to be wealthy.

Stephen's father, George, formed a partnership with his aunt (his mother's sister) and together they built an apartment building. George purchased the land, constructed the building and then sold it. George had learned that he could build the apartment building for the cost of the mortgage on the family home, and so he sold the family home and invested the money in another apartment building. Thirty years after all this started, and son Stephen had graduated from college, George owned more than half a dozen residential apartment buildings. One day, George had had enough; he felt insulted when one of his tenants had demanded a new stove. He had grown tired of having to deal with residential tenants, so he sold all of the buildings and re-invested in commercial real estate, under the impression that commercial space would be less of a headache to manage.

By the time Stephen joined the family business, the family had accumulated a real estate portfolio worth more than $800 million. Stephen basically joined the business to try and protect staff from his father. He felt the need to become the staff's protector. Stephen shared that he had developed the "special files" so that the company could pay all of the bills that George didn't want to pay. His mom would go into the ladies washroom and sign all of the checks required to pay these overdue bills. Meanwhile, George thought if he tore up the bills he didn't want to pay, that they would simply disappear. He just had this thing about not paying bills.

Based upon his upbringing and how he had witnessed his father behaving with money and people in general, Stephen developed a Money Motto™ which he described thus: "Money makes problems go away!"

On the surface, this might appear to be a fairly healthy Money Motto,™ yet when we examined how Stephen's Money Motto™ impacted his relationships, what we discovered was quite the opposite. The price of one's Money Motto™ are the consequences of how one feels and hence behaves with respect to money and wealth. For Stephen, the price he was paying for his Money Motto™ was that he operated on the assumption that money cures all problems and consequently he does not have to get emotionally involved in any transaction. With this fundamental belief,

Stephen's tendency was to throw money at problems in his life, in the hope that money would always prove to be the resolution.

When we examined how this belief system was negatively influencing his relationships, Stephen realized that what he had been doing had not only been detrimental to him, it had actually created far more serious problems. These problems were not of a nature that could easily be resolved; typically, over time, the problems simply grew in magnitude. This became most evident when we examined the relationship Stephen had with his son, Jeremy.

Having worked with Stephen for quite a number of months, together we had uncovered what mattered most to him, identified the kind of legacy he wanted to leave behind and confirmed the damaging nature of his Money Motto.™ Stephen became quite aware of the fact that he had done much over the years to contribute to the creation of a "spoiled brat" in his son Jeremy's attitude towards his father, the family business, and his own unbridled sense of entitlement.

A Son's Perspective

> *If you don't like something, change it.*
> *If you can't change it, change your attitude.*
> — MAYA ANGELOU —

Jeremy has a serious dilemma. He is wealthy, enjoys the benefits his wealth provides, yet he is resentful of the wealth to which he has access. In working together, Jeremy was able to distinguish with clarity the source of his resentment. Seeing his grandfather belittle his own staff and son, his father, Stephen, Jeremy associated wealth with his feelings for his grandfather because it was his grandfather who initially built up the real estate empire. Jeremy appears to have inherited his grandfather's anger and, as a result, he has become a bully. Whenever he loses his temper, he treats others just as his grandfather did.

Under the estate plan the family presently has in place, the shares of the company are to be evenly disbursed among four grandchildren—Jeremy being one of the four—and all of them cousins to each other. All of the cousins presently work in the business in one capacity or another. The oldest grandchild is the current CEO of the business and has been working on creating a role for Jeremy. This, despite the fact that Jeremy has a deep resentment towards the business that he cannot separate from his resentment over how his grandfather treated his father. Together, we were able to clarify his Money Motto™ as: "I am angry at and resentful of my money."

When together we examined how his Money Motto™ is having a negative influence in Jeremy's life, he was able recognize how tormented and torn he felt in swinging back and forth between his resentment of his money and wealth and appreciation and enjoyment of the lifestyle it affords him. In examining how it impacts his relationships with his cousins, Jeremy was able to see that he harbors resentments towards them as well. With respect to how his Money Motto™ impacts his relationship with the family business and his role as a shareholder, Jeremy now realizes how it holds him back from being able to freely contribute without the resentment he holds towards his grandfather—who built the business—from always surfacing.

Given too, how his grandfather treated Stephen, he developed the Money Motto™: "Money makes problems go away!" Stephen allows his son to bully him. Stephen realized he has rarely ever said "no" to his son, or ever denied him anything.

Here we are with a son who resents his wealth, is angry at his grandfather for treating his father poorly and angry at his father for letting him get away with his own mistreatment of him. As if this were not sufficiently complicated, we have a father who cannot say "no" to his son, and is still planning on bequeathing all of his wealth to a son who resents money!

Stephen is presently in the midst of his estate planning, and his advisors are busy looking at what is the most tax-efficient strategy for passing on as much wealth to Jeremy (who resents money) as they can find. The problem is, none of these advisors know this, because they have not identified or in any way become aware of the Great White Elephants that exist in this family. So, here we are in the process of giving more money to someone who resents it and I'm forced to ask: Is this a responsible thing to be doing?

How does Stephen learn to stand up to his son and say "no," at least occasionally, and thereafter work on developing an emotional connection with his son? What must Jeremy do so he can let go of his resentment over his wealth and find a way to embrace the gift that it really represents? How can he become more comfortable and at ease with being a part of the family business and contribute to its growth for future generations with his cousins? How do we address these Great White Elephants, and take them into consideration during the balance of the estate planning process, as opposed to naming them and ignoring them as simply a hindrance to the tabletop discussions?

The process we undertook with Jeremy was basically the same as we undertook with Hal, Lizzy, and Victor. Allow me to recap the five stages in the process:

1. Clarity
2. Congruency
3. Connection
4. Conversation
5. Commitment

Jeremy had to get clear on his core value (Humility), his "why," and uncover his Money Motto:™ "I am resentful of the money I have." He also had to become aware of the impact of his core value and Money Motto™ on his relationships. Once all of this had been achieved, Jeremy had to start to behave in a way that his actions were in alignment with his core value, his "why" so that he could experience a new, congruent way of being. This new way of being had to be applied in all of his relationships, especially the one he had with his father and those with his three cousins. Once this new pattern of interaction was launched and under way, Jeremy had to make room for some forgiveness—for himself, his father, and his grandfather.

We continued to support Jeremy with coaching on how to have the right conversations, the right way, so that Jeremy was able to take responsibility for his past actions and behaviors, all while working on making amends and asking for forgiveness. This represents a lot of heavy, emotional work, but it was from such a place that Jeremy was able to develop a new set of commitments to guide his future actions and behavior. All in all, Jeremy ends up creating a new way of being; one which is congruent and fully aligned with his "why."

In being open to some serious personal reflection and introspection, coaching and change management, and extending his trust to us to follow the process that we advocated, Jeremy was able to face up to and let go of his perception of how he felt about money and the family business. It is very important for individuals in business families to identify and face their Great White Elephants regarding money and wealth. If they do not do this, then the beast will "remain in the room" always present, and forever getting in the way, undermining anyone's ability to truly enjoy and celebrate the gift that has been bestowed on them by their parents or grandparents. With the elephant in the room, under the table, the unspoken challenges surrounding ownership, power, money and wealth will always be in play.

The Top Ten Challenges of Wealth

Troubles are a lot like people—they grow bigger if you nurse them.
— UNKNOWN —

You have worked hard to earn and build your wealth, and although you were smart enough to know it would not always be plain sailing thereafter, you were not prepared nor did you expect it to be as hard as it has been. Knowing about how your wealth really affects you and your family on a personal level, and how your attitudes towards wealth have evolved, all mean that you can hope to manage it well—both technically and emotionally—and ultimately give yourself far more control, success, and satisfaction.

Our firm conducted a survey to explore how people felt about their money and wealth. We wanted to try and reveal the most significant challenges that wealth represents from the perspective of those who are wealthy. Furthermore, we wanted to discover the greatest fears harbored by wealthy parents who know their children will some day inherit the wealth they have spent a working lifetime to establish.

Our survey revealed the following as the top ten challenges of having wealth:

1. Guilt
2. Fear of responsibility
3. Sense of entitlement
4. Above the law and/or society
5. Burdened or ashamed
6. Disconnected from reality
7. Isolated and lonely
8. Misusing it to control or manipulate others
9. Undermining the personal drive of beneficiaries
10. Being taken advantage of personally

The most significant fear that wealthy parents have is over whether they have they done a proper job in preparing the next generation to inherit their wealth. Here's the catch: parents don't have clarity over what they mean by properly or adequately preparing their children, nor can they successfully articulate what being prepared looks like in practical terms. I ask you to recall the Ferrari analogy in the Introduction.

As a society, we struggle with these challenges because we have not been preparing our children to inherit wealth. This is because the succession planning and wealth transition industry has been focused on the quantitative side of money and wealth, and pays little or no attention to the fact that every one of us, as human beings, has a emotional relationship with money—our Money Motto.™ Our Money Motto™ will influence how we behave in relationship with our spouse or life partner, to the other members of our family, to those at work and in our business activities—our colleagues and co-workers, to our friends and acquaintances, and throughout our various communities of interaction, including our voluntary and charitable works, even into our succession and wealth transition plans. Our Money Motto™ also influences how we make our most significant financial decisions such as how we earn our money, negotiate for it, and bequeath it to the next generation. It is, therefore, an invaluable investment to take some time to uncover and understand the impact your Money Motto™ has in your life and the decisions you make on a daily basis, so you can be fully prepared meet these challenges and face down all of your Great White Elephants as they relate to money and wealth.

Here are three things you might want to consider doing soon, if not right away:

1. Identify your core values, which are a collection of guiding principles—usually positive ones—that govern your personal conduct and you feel to be both proper and desirable for you to follow throughout your life.

2. Identify your current Money Motto™ and determine whether it is empowering or holding you back from living in alignment your stated core values. Core values usually don't change, but they are refined and become more focused as you grow older. It is our beliefs about and behaviors around money (our personal Money Motto™) that must change if we are to live in alignment with our core values which means we can live a life of purpose and make our contributions in a way that is congruent with our core values.

3. Develop a new Money Motto™ that is congruent with your core values. This will diminish the challenges of having money and wealth and help instill a new perspective on how you feel about your money and wealth.

Questions to Ponder...

1. Was money discussed at the kitchen table growing up?

2. What was the context: was it negative or positive?

3. How do you use money to control your children?

4. How does money define you?

5. What are you not teaching your children about money?

6. What is your Great White Elephant™ as it relates to money?

5

FINDING OUR POWER IN THE MISSING CONVERSATION

A man's character is his fate.

— KEVIN KLINE as Mr. Hundred, in the movie *The Emperor's Club* —

What's Your White Elephant? The Currents Under the Table

We must be the change we wish to see in the world.

— MAHATMA GANDHI —

AS HUMAN BEINGS, WHEN THINGS DO NOT WORK OUT in the way we had hoped, one of our natural tendencies inclines us towards blaming others, the situation, or perhaps, worse, ourselves. As I write this final chapter of the book, I find myself in exactly this predicament. The woman with whom—until recently—I had been in a relationship and had planned on spending the rest of my life with—broke up with me! The pain I find myself experiencing is, at times, almost unbearable. My stomach hurts, as if someone repeatedly punched it; of the little food I am eating right now, it is either bland or tasteless; and I judge myself to be drinking too much, hoping the wine and liquor will help erase the pain. As if this wasn't enough, I experience my mind racing with thoughts and memories of the past and all the good times we had spent together.

I blame myself for the break-up. If only I had been more courageous and honest from the outset, we might still be together. If only I had not been so needy, clingy, and insecure, maybe we still might be together. If only, if only, if only…

Last night, I felt a pull to watch *The Emperor's Club* again, starring Kevin Kline. The movie is about a history teacher and his students. It is a story about honor and integrity. Very early in the movie, Mr. Hundred is reflecting on his tenure as a teacher, the impact he has had on his students, and how he has made a contribution—or not—to the development of their character. "A man's character is his fate," he thinks… as he reflects.

I find myself pondering this quote. "A man's character is his fate." Being the inquisitive type that I am, I ask myself what part of my own character has contributed to produce the outcome—the demise of this relationship—that I am now facing? Sitting with this question for a couple of months, drew me to the following conclusion—my current undisclosed Great White Elephant.™

At a fundamental level, I do not feel safe, or believe I am sufficiently valuable or worthy to be deserving of the good things I do have in my life; things like the love of a beautiful, powerful woman, wealth, fame, success, ease of existence, and the ability to make a difference to my fellow human beings. I believe that I am worthless, of no importance, have no value, am too different, and so if I open up my mouth or try to express myself I will be made fun of, laughed at, ridiculed, and bullied.

Our negative, self-destructive thoughts are Great White Elephants in our lives. They are Great White Elephants because most the time—although we are not necessarily always conscious of these thoughts—they will always have an impact on how we see ourselves, how we behave towards ourselves, contributing to a poor self-image and lowering our self-esteem. They are like the background music in an elevator. Next time you find yourself in an elevator, quiet your mind and listen; the music will be there, just like your subconscious thoughts and insecurities.

It is really important that we identify these thoughts and see them as our Great White Elephants, take ownership of them, and those that don't serve us well—which will be the majority of them—toss them out! As an individual who is either already doing great things or who seeks to achieve still greater things in your life, you don't have the luxury of hanging on to these Great White Elephants any longer. Later in this chapter, I propose the concept that our thoughts are not real—that they are just expressions of our ego.

I want to share with you some of my own Great White Elephants, the negative self-talk scripts that used to run my life. With beliefs like the ones I've listed above—as the constant music in my head—what I have done and continue to do to surmount them, or conquer them, is to overcompensate. In order for me to fulfill this need I have to prove that I am successful and hence valuable, I confuse being successful with being valuable. I have it in my head that if I am successful—by some external definition of what success should be or should look like—then I will by default, be seen and regarded by others as valuable. At a subconscious level, I make decisions to sacrifice a part of myself to achieve this perception of success, so I can feel and look valuable to others.

In working with my coach and mentor, Dov Baron, as we examine how I behave in relationships and what it is I do in relationships to explain my behavior, Dov presents the concept and phrase he coined: "othering myself." Through my work with Dov, I have become present to the fact that I felt emotionally abandoned when I was a child. The impact this still has on me as an adult is one of feeling I don't quite belong or feel I have as strong a sense of belonging as I think I should, and this fuels my sense of not feeling valuable to others. When I choose to pursue an intimate relationship, I appear to pick ones in which I will either be abandoned or I will end up doing the abandoning; this behavior feeds the original childhood wounds and keeps the mind believing that I am not valuable, feeding my Great White Elephant.™

Here's the important learning for me: I abandoned myself in this relationship. After my most recent break-up, and after a lot of journaling about it, I got to see how I contributed to this outcome.

First of all, I was not behaving with complete integrity and, at some point in the relationship, I abandoned myself and became lost in the relationship. I vanished. As Dov puts it, "I othered myself" for the relationship, so I would not feel abandoned. The result, I abandoned myself (by not behaving with complete integrity). Effectively, I gave my power away.

In the context of the topic of this book, I would like you to consider power, from the perspective of your thoughts and feelings and what you give away as a result of such thoughts and feelings. It is your thoughts and feelings that will dictate how you handle power as an owner and a beneficiary. What does power mean to you? In the example I shared about my personal relationship, power meant being vulnerable (behaving with complete integrity). I gave away my power of being vulnerable by letting my Great White Elephant™—my thoughts and feelings of being unsafe and not valuable—control and run away with me, instead of letting my power of being valuable guide me and speak the truth.

At this point in the book, I would like you to consider the following question: "Where have YOU othered yourself and for what?" Another way to present this question is: "What powers have you given away?" Think of this in the context of your family business. Has the business become your identity? Are you in the business to please your father, grandfather, or someone else other than yourself?

There is a part of us, the most valuable part of us, that we give away when we other ourselves. We give away our power; our power or capacity to be true to ourselves and to respect and love ourselves; our power to be authentic and congruent in all our thoughts and actions, our power to speak the truth and act with integrity. We end up giving ourselves away in pursuit of what we think we really want and it's all an over compensation for some unfulfilled emotional need. I have seen this same sort of dynamic played out in many client families who own a business enterprise, and especially during the succession planning and wealth transfer process.

A Son's Desire to Please his Father

You can clutch the past so tightly to your chest,
that it leaves your arms too full to embrace the present.
— JAN GLIDEWELL —

Trent is an example of such a story. His father would always tell Trent: "One day you will have the opportunity to be the breadwinner for this family and you will do this by assuming responsibility for running the family business, by taking over that role from me." Having heard this plan for most of his young life, Trent felt he had an obligation to assume the responsibility for running the family business in order to be the breadwinner. Being a pleaser by nurture, a trait Trent learned from an early age, if he were ever to succeed in receiving his father's attention, he had to do things that clearly pleased his father. Over time, it is not surprising that Trent convinced himself that what was expected of him and had always been expected of him—to end up running the family business—was the only thing he ever wanted to do himself.

Trent was introduced to me by one of his friends, who had seen him struggle with the relationship Trent has with his father. In our initial conversations, Trent shared his concerns about the lack of authenticity in his relationship with himself as well as that with his father. He felt that his father had never really been interested in him or his desire to pursue the arts and become a performer. As a result of his father's disinterest and the underlying belief that his son could never support himself financially with his ideal choice of vocation, Trent was left with a deep feeling of insecurity and doubt over his own abilities and right to follow his heart and pursue his own passions and what he felt was his true calling.

In working together, Trent was able to identify, among other insights, his Money Motto™ as: "Money is a measure of success." This motto played out in his life because he identified his father with success, and therefore money with his father. Since Trent harbored such a deep resentment towards his father, and he was struggling financially, Trent was blaming his father for his own lack of success, instead of owning the fact that he was actually sabotaging his opportunities for success, and for making money in his chosen career. Trent believed if he were to actually experience success and make any money he would end up becoming his father—and the very same kind of person he had long resented.

Once Trent was able to see the impact of his Money Motto,™ he chose to take responsibility for his own lack of authenticity in his relationship with his father. He was able to share his Money Motto™ with his father and explain the impact it had on him and their relationship. Trent was able to articulate how money had created a separation between the two of them from a very young age. Trent told his father that he had been intimidated by money and success, both of which for him, had come to represent everything his father stood for, and therefore by extension, Trent had felt intimidated by his father, the family business and his own sense of insecurity and failure—in not being able to be the son he thought his father wanted.

After healing his relationship with his father, Trent was able to understand how his Money Motto™ had held him back from becoming successful in his chosen career. With further coaching, Trent was able to recreate his Money Motto™ as: "It's okay to follow my passion and make money doing something I love." The new motto empowered him to re-launch his career as a performer and turn it into a profitable vocation. From this new platform of success, Trent went on to develop a business that was supported by his passion for performance arts.

For most of us, how we feel about money and wealth has the potential to be a Great White Elephant™ and have a negative impact in our lives. Most of us have never really taken the time to clarify the answer we might offer to the simple question: How do we feel about money?; let alone have any awareness of the impact our feelings have on ourselves and others. As I shared Trent's story, did it raise any thoughts or feelings about where you might be blaming someone else for your own—real or perceived—lack of success?

Diagnostics:
The Art of Asking Powerful Questions

The quality of your life depends on the
quality of the questions you ask yourself.
— THELMA BOX —

As I tell all my clients, when they are still in the process of considering whether to hire me, "if you are looking to me for your answers, then I'm definitely the wrong guy for you. However, I do believe that we all have our own best answers inside us, we have just never been asked—or asked ourselves—the right questions." The challenge is what does one do with those answers, once you have discovered what they are? I also tend to think that most people know what the answers are for resolving the issues they are facing in their lives; they are just not ready to face them, or implement them, so they actually avoid asking the obvious questions out loud.

Deep down inside, most of us, most of the time, know what to do. When we do not act, for whatever reason, perhaps because we have not found the necessary courage, or perhaps the pain or discomfort, or di-ease, is not yet sufficiently painful enough for us to act or behave differently, then we proceed as we have always done.

There is much in life that causes us distress and discomfort, and it is enough for us to get conscious and be real with ourselves. However, if we look below the surface, and really see with an open heart and with all our soul, the possibilities for life-transforming lessons run deep, and it is here that we really learn about true power, real responsibility, love, hope, and our own honesty and authenticity.

Life becomes clear when we have the courage to face our Great White Elephants by asking the right questions and dealing with the answers in a powerful way that is aligned with who we are and what we are really meant to do with our life. We think that we are being powerful when we resist and withhold our emotions and don't express who we really want to be. We think our power comes from being who we think we should or ought to be and by what we do, instead of being honest with others and ourselves. When we are not honest with others, or ourselves, we give all of our authentic power away.

I now see how I gave all of my own authentic power away in my last intimate relationship. I was not behaving with complete integrity; I withheld thoughts, feelings, and facts. As I look back, I realize I was afraid that if I had behaved with complete integrity she would leave me. The irony is that by not behaving with complete integrity she left me anyway. I did not get what I wanted, which was an open and trusting relationship. I share this with you because I would like you to examine where you are not behaving with complete integrity with others or with yourself.

Take an integrity inventory in your life. Ask yourself: Where are you being inauthentic with yourself and with others. What do I mean by being inauthentic? I mean not being honest with yourself and others about whatever is important to you. Telling the truth and nothing but the truth—your own truth—is what's required. Consider all areas of your life and all of your significant relationships, including your intimate relationships, with yourself, your spouse, partner, or significant other, and your children; your relationships with your immediate and extended family, including your father, mother, grandfathers and grandmothers, uncles, aunts and cousins. Next examine the relationship you have with your work and business, your investments and other assets, and your other material possessions.

In asking ourselves what I collectively call the "obvious questions," and through being completely genuine with ourselves, we are able to develop a much clearer vision of our current reality and what is really going on in the here and now. Once we have a clear picture of our current reality, we can superimpose that current reality over our desired reality—our dreams, desires, and goals.

The process can be arduous and time-consuming since it involves a one-on-one interview/conversation with each member of your family—in private—to obtain a similarly clear picture of their own current reality, as it relates to them and the rest of the family; and for each individual, we superimpose their current reality with their own desired reality and their stated dreams, desires, and goals. By asking each family member for their own, unique and personal perspective, we find that most of our clients who have participated with us in this process have commented that for the most part, they have really felt heard for the first time in their lives, and have some greater measure of hope that long-sought after changes might actually take place.

One of the most frequently voiced complaints I hear from clients is that the family has engaged the services of all sorts of consultants, who came, interviewed, reported, and then billed, and yet nothing of significance changed! I think I have discovered the reason for this commonly reported outcome. I believe the members of the client family, and all the consultants, are equally responsible for the lack of change because they avoided asking the awkward, difficult and obvious questions and consequently did not raise or discuss the Great White Elephants residing within the family. There could be myriad reasons for this sort of outcome and none of them really matter. The point is that the right conversations did not happen. In one of the films from the *Star Wars* series, Yoda the Jedi knight—who is a hero of mine— tells young Luke Skywalker: "Do or do not. There is no try."

We either have the courage to acknowledge our Great White Elephants or not. Once we have acknowledged them, all we can ask ourselves is what are we willing to do about them?

The first step in our private practice process is to develop a Diagnostic Report for our clients. I like to describe this process and the resulting document as the equivalent of experiencing a full physical examination at the Mayo Clinic except our process focuses on values, beliefs, patterns of behavior, goals, desires, and objectives, all taken from an emotional perspective.

On the next two pages, there is an example of a Diagnostic Report prepared for the matriarch of a client family. Jo-Anna was referred to us by her accountant, who had concerns that Jo-Anna's children were all lacking in any personal focus and drive because their mother, Jo-Anna, was making life too easy for them. She was funding each of her children's lifestyle without any of them doing anything to actually earn the lifestyle she was providing.

Once we reviewed the results of Jo-Anna's Diagnostic Report with her, she became very much aware of her Great White Elephant™ of excessive generosity towards her children and all because of her own underlying beliefs about money. Jo-Anna grew up being taken care of by her father, and subsequently her older brother who now heads the family business. Jo-Anna's default and automatic response and way of doing things is to look after those she loves, just as she was taken care of. What the Diagnostic Report pointed out was the cost to Jo-Anna in doing this and her perpetuation of the family pattern of behavior with similarly

DESIRED REALITY	CURRENT REALITY
To provide the next generation with tools on how to handle money responsibly so they can be independent and comfortable in dealing with money and wealth.	Children are dependent and have no sense of responsibility about money.
For the next generation to have an emotional awareness of money and understand their relationship with it (how to use it, how to take care of it so that it may take care of them).	There is a lack of clarity on how the children feel about being wealthy and appear not to be taking care of the money that is given to them. Therefore they are not prepared to inherit wealth.
For the next generation to be clear about their values and have aligned their relationship with money with their values.	Children do not understand their emotional relationship with money and the potential risks that are present if this is not addressed.
To have the next generation motivated, focused, and clear on what they want to do and how to achieve it.	Children have no sense of direction. Their ambition has been kneecapped.

DESIRED REALITY	CURRENT REALITY
For the next generation to be wise, responsible, and charitable with their money. For them to respect it by not squandering it.	Children do not have the emotional wisdom to be responsible around money therefore they do not respect it.
To have a formal structure and process in place to pass on wealth with clearly defined boundaries and consequences for the next generation.	There is no formal structure or process in place. Therefore there are no boundaries to protect the G2s or the G3s from each other's expectations.
For the next generation to recognize their cousins as potential business partners and to realize the opportunities that money and wealth can provide and be in position to take advantage of this.	There is no motivation or drive on the part of the children.
For the next generation to be clear on their sense of purpose and contribution, which will fuel their drive to contribute to the family and to the community.	Children are not contributing to the family or community.

destructive results in undermining her own children's personal focus, drive, and ambition for their own future.

Beliefs: Our Reality and Our Perception

You have to learn to select your thoughts,
like you select your clothes, everyday.
— UNKNOWN —

In Chapter 3, I discussed the concepts of thought, feeling, being, and how life works in being both simple and complex. We have thoughts, and these lead to feelings and, as a result, we have a way of being, a way of behaving and experiencing life, which in turn creates our reality. Another way to say this is what you conceive, think and feel, you create; what you create you experience, what you experience you create.

What you have in your life and the circumstances you are in have been your creation as a result of the thoughts and feelings you have had. I know this is hard to accept at first. Some of you might be saying I don't like what I have or I am not happy with my current situation. Know this: This is only your current reality. You have the power and capability to create a new reality, your desired reality. You set about changing your current reality and circumstances by being aware of your thoughts and feelings.

Know this too: You have a right to your happiness and joy. Thoughts are like magnets, drawing circumstances and situations to you. The most difficult thing for people to do is to listen to their own heart. Learn what your heart desires and follow your heart's desire. You will know what this is because you will feel joy, excitement, and bliss. We often judge ourselves for wanting what we want, and we consider ourselves wrong for wanting what we want. We can convince ourselves that the things we want are bad for us and, not only do we not deserve them, we too must be bad for wanting them.

Our thoughts can and do create much of our our reality. However, our thoughts are not the entirety of our reality. They are just thoughts, nothing else and they are not real. We perceive what we think of as real. For example, I have thoughts that I am not safe, because of some insecurity stemming from being bullied as a child. The reality is that I am safe most of the time, and many times I feel unsafe because of a thought that might have been triggered by a recent event, which reminded me of the past event, and consequently I feel I'm not safe. So, does it not make sense to be aware of and monitor our thoughts? We can confuse our thoughts and allow them to color and shape our reality.

I recall having thoughts in a recent romantic relationship that I was not worthy of love and didn't deserve to have such a beautiful woman as an intimate partner. Is this true? Of course not! I am worthy of love and I do deserve a beautiful woman as an intimate partner. What I have learned is that I must have positive thoughts, so that I may create a positive outcome as a reality. I am in control of my destiny, as are you. We have the power to write our story; the pen is in our hands. Nothing is being done to you, all things are created by you, and this is an outcome of your thoughts. With this, there can be no more victims or the ability to blame, as you are accountable for creating your reality, all as a result of your thoughts.

While attending a leadership program, I became aware of a thought or script that has influenced me for a long time. The thought was/is, that I don't feel safe—for whatever reason, I'm unsure. The leader of the program posed this question to me: "Am I really not safe, or is it just a thought?" He asked me to take a walk with this question for the next 24 hours and try and become really aware of what was going on for me when the thought of being unsafe came to mind and, when it did, to ask myself the following question: "Am I safe?"

As much as possible, I spent the following 24 hours in New York City as if I were a third-party, trying to maintain some detachment from myself, as I focused on trying to remain present to my own thoughts and resulting feelings. It astonished me how frequently I had the thought that I didn't feel safe. In asking myself the question the leader had suggested, I was more able to recognize and feel that I was indeed safe, and that this was simply a thought I was having, nothing more. It was a very powerful experience for me. The results of my experiencing this breakthrough have been profound. I now live from a much different perspective, one in which I am safe. While the same thoughts never completely go away, I find I now have the ability to recognize when the thought is present, and turn the volume down a little more promptly.

Before I had this breakthrough experience, I had to become aware of my Great White Elephant™ regarding this particular thought and insecurity and see it for what it was, just a thought. The next step was learning to ask myself the obvious question (Am I really not safe?) and then be prepared to engage in the third step that is about being responsible and personally accountable for my thoughts and behaviors and how they can influence what subsequently happens in my life.

Being Accountable: Facing Your Fear Responsibly

> To change one's life: Start immediately.
> Do it flamboyantly. No exceptions!
> — WILLIAM JAMES —

What does it mean to accountable and responsible? I think being accountable is to take responsibility for our past behaviors, and being responsible is being committed to building a new way of being. I see them as irrevocably linked.

For the purposes of what is being discussed here, I consider being accountable and responsible to mean becoming authentic about your in-authenticity; it means apologizing for any instance where one has not been authentic or real with another person or indeed with yourself. It is also about recommitting to whatever you are committed to in any relationship, whether that is the relationship you have with yourself or with another person.

Most people enter into relationships, any kind of relationship, and focus on whatever it is they expect to gain—fulfilling their own expectations—as opposed to being intentional about what they might give to the relationship. By nature, we tend towards selfish, self-serving behavior, putting ourselves and our own needs before those of others.

In the movie *Eat, Pray, Love* there is a powerful scene that I think depicts this notion of accountability and responsibility. It is about a missing conversation. The character Liz Gilbert, played by Julia Roberts, is in Italy and she is about to sit down to a beautiful lunch she prepared for herself and, in the same moment, she gains some insight/clarity about her boyfriend, who is back home in New York City.

This is what she writes in a letter to her boyfriend (as she feels for him):

> "We acknowledge we have screwed up this relationship and yet we stick it out anyway; we both accept we fight a lot, and don't want to live without each other, this way, we can spend the rest of our lives together, be miserable but also happy that we are not apart."

In her letter, she describes the Augustium, built by emperor Octavius Augustus to house his bodily remains. Throughout its existence/history, it has survived many onslaughts by barbarians and now lies in ruins. At some point, during the Dark Ages, the emperor's ashes were stolen. In the twelfth century it became a fortress for the Collona family, later a bullring, and then, a warehouse for fireworks. Today it has become something of an unofficial home for many of Rome's homeless people.

It is also one of the quietest and loneliest places in Rome, and it feels like a precious wound or heartbreak you can't let go of, because the hurt is all too familiar and difficult to let go of. We all want things to stay the same. We settle for living in misery because we are afraid of change and things crumbling to ruins. When I looked around at this place (the Augustium) and the chaos it has endured, the way it has been adapted, burned, pillaged and found a way to build itself back up again, I was reassured that maybe my life has not been so chaotic; really, it is just the world that is chaotic and the real trap is getting attached to any of it. A state of ruin is really a gift. A state of ruin is a necessary step on the road to transformation.

Julia's character describes that being in the Augustium shows her that we must be prepared for endless waves of transformation, and both she and her boyfriend deserve something better than staying together because they are afraid they will be destroyed if they don't.

Based on my own experiences, I believe that if we find the courage to have the missing conversations they will initially lead to a sense of ruin. What I have also become aware of, having faced up to my own missing conversations, is that ruin eventually becomes the road to transformation. The missing conversations (and the source of many Great White Elephants in our lives) are those we are afraid to have, because we fear the outcome of the conversation may cause ruin from which we cannot recover or rebuild. Because we are often stuck and made immoveable by our fear and our thoughts of being afraid, the fear actually ends up controlling us and keeps us from being more honest, authentic and real.

The result is we "other" ourselves because of our fear over having the missing conversation. What we don't realize is that by having the courage to engage in the missing conversation we set ourselves free and, in the process find and reclaim our power. The outcome we can look forward to, in finding the courage to have the missing conversation, is a greater love and deeper connection with others, as well as for and with ourselves. Having the missing conversation, facing your Great White Elephant,™ actually sets you free; free to be more aligned with your authentic self without constraints or limitations; free to love those that matter to you the most; especially free to love yourself.

Loving Ourselves:
It's What We are Really Searching For

Love is, above all, the gift of oneself.

— JEAN ANOUILH —

If we are brave enough to leave the comfortable and familiar behind—and this could mean leaving our thoughts and ideas, our relationships, and all of our material possessions behind—and risk the misunderstanding, lack of forgiveness and resentment of others, while we embark on a truth-seeking journey (both internally and externally) with a willingness to accept that everything that happens does so for a reason, and where everyone we meet has something to teach us, and we are prepared to face up to and then forgive ourselves for all our faults and shortcomings, then the truth shall not be withheld from us.

Our power is in our truth. Our truth is whatever we choose to say it is. We create it. This is our authentic power, the power to create what we want, intentionally aligned with what matters most to us. Our truth is also our promise to ourselves. Our truth is *our* promise.

In a recent conversation with a dear friend of mine, he was sharing with me the first time he took his two boys to watch *Batman Returns*. They were on the edge of their seats as they watched the movie. About six months later, they watched the movie again for the second time. After watching the movie for the second time my friend shared with me that he had a conversation with his boys and asked them about what was different for them in the experience of having watched the movie for a second time. The boys commented that there was less drama and anxiety as a result of experiencing the movie the second time. They had already watched the movie and knew how it would end.

I would like you to consider that you have the tools, your truth to define how your own movie ends. Since you already know the ending of your movie (whatever it may be, perhaps the outcome of your succession plan, how your children will handle the ownership, power, and money) there will be less drama and anxiety.

I now know this to be true, for I have found my own truth. My truth is that I am safe and valuable. As a result of finding and claiming my own truth, I have, in turn, become a safe place for those I serve and love. I am also seen as valuable by my clients as I assist them in finding their own truth and help them to embrace the feeling of safety they also have within themselves. I have experienced a change in how I glide through life. My life has an ease and certainty to it, my truth.

For a significant part of my life, I have believed that I had little value and rarely felt safe. I found my truth as a result of being recently single. It was a new place for me and I was forced to face some difficult realities about myself. When my girlfriend broke up with me, I was devastated, and had to face my fear of being alone. I did not know what to do with myself. I would keep myself busy with work, focusing on writing this book, or anything else to avoid being alone with myself and my thoughts.

I recall a recent homeward-bound trip after an extensive business trip. I'm flying into Vancouver and become increasingly aware of the loneliness I feel in returning to an empty house. I actually dreaded the thought of going home and being by myself. I had to face this fear and, in doing just that, was able to find myself and my truth; the truth of who I am, no longer willing to pretend to be anyone other than my authentic self. When I am in control of my personal power, it is impossible to "other" myself for anything or anyone else.

What I have become comfortable with is the notion that I feel okay hanging out all by myself. I enjoy being with myself. I've realized I can just be and not have to be constantly doing. It is in the being that I get to experience my true authentic self (safe and valuable). In simply being with myself, I'm finding I am getting to know myself at a deeper level, in a richer way. I feel have a greater clarity about who I am and an improved awareness of my Great White Elephants. All of this provides me with a new approach through which I can connect or check in with myself which includes getting to know all of me—the good and beautiful, the bad and ugly, the insecurities, and the power. This has enabled me to live my life with some greater congruency. In being present to and with myself, I can monitor the conversations that occur in my head, and I have the power, through my truth, to change or transform these conversations into different, more empowering conversations, which help me to renew my commitments about how I will choose to live my life.

Here's something I became aware of just the other day. I got present to how I become stressed over money, and what I think about, I subsequently create. Now, when I think about money, instead of becoming stressed, I replace that response with a feeling of joy and ease with money, and replace the old tape of: "I have to work hard for my money." to "Money comes easily and frequently."

Our truth is what we most earnestly seek. But to find it, we must go on a journey and search for it. As I have found out in the past and more recently as a result of my circumstances, we must take the journey alone into our own Augustium, so we can transform ourselves as a result of experiencing a state of ruin. Ruin is the road to transformation, no matter how painful the road may sometimes be. Eventually, beauty comes out of ruin. I have given myself permission to experience more emotions in the last six months than I have hithertofore experienced throughout my life. I do mean a full range of emotions too: from deep, passionate love, agonizing hurt, blissful joy, profound sadness and regret, and serenity. My truth as I am discovering it, because it is a work in progress, is: "I am safe and valuable." As a dear friend of mine said: "Franco when you get that you are safe and valuable, you will be unstoppable!" I now know and feel this to be true. I wrote this book to change the succession planning industry and your life, so that you may find your truth.

Do you remember Hal from Chapter 1? He is also a seeker of truth. In working together, Hal was able to clarify that he is not wholly defined by his thoughts but that they still accounted for some of his Great White Elephants that, at times, he allows to frame his worldview, and the way he lives his life.

Part of the coaching process involved my asking Hal to name his truth or, to put it another way, his promise to himself. As individuals, we are forever making promises to ourselves or to loved-ones, promises we very often fail to fulfill. This sort of failure or shortcoming both frustrates and disempowers us as well as the person to whom we made the promise. We all get caught in making promises to do something and then fall short, or we make similar overtures to stop doing something else, and blithely continue to keep doing it. Our behavior doesn't change sufficiently for us to make good on our promises.

During the course of a Landmark Leadership program I attended, the facilitator asked us participants the following question: "What if, instead of being a person with a promise, the person is the promise?"

What if I am my promise, instead of being a man with a promise? A man with a promise which I will more than likely break—based on my past experience, track record, and the present state of my life; incidentally, I am not trying to make myself wrong here or intent on beating myself up, I'm just stating the facts as I see them.

The next question we were asked was: "What is your promise?" I like to ask this same question in the following way: "What's *your* truth?"

Returning to my work with Hal, I asked him what his promise to himself would be, moving forward. What came up for him was: Lovable. Hal realized that he has been lovable to everybody around him, but not towards himself. As he realized this, he immediately felt a sadness and regret for all that had occurred in his life and, as a result, immediately went to a place of blame and wrongdoing (the Great White Elephant™ is in the house). I gently reminded Hal that the thoughts don't go away, but that he has some greater awareness, as well as a new tool—the promise he made to himself— that can be used as a volume control when the negative thoughts return and threaten to derail him.

The question Hal chose to ask himself whenever his Great White Elephants return, was: "What would lovable do now?" In other words, what would be the loving thing for Hal to do now? Asking the question will help silence and disempower the Great White Elephant™ and the answer you need to address the issue or deal with the situation will become clear. Form your new resolve.

The 5 C's of Great White Elephant™ Busting!

I have shared many stories, some personal and some from among the clients in my private practice. We developed a simple methodology, the essence of which has been followed by all of our client participants; I've followed the same pattern myself. It is a methodology I shared at the outset, in the Introduction to this book. There are five steps that, if properly integrated into your business succession and wealth transfer planning, will greatly improve your odds of success. Moving diligently through these five steps will mean that you and your children are fully prepared—both intellectually and emotionally—to bequeath and inherit ownership, power, and money. These five steps or processes are the Great White Elephant™ busters! It is important to point out that these steps must be worked through in the same order as they have been presented and in the way we intended for you to work through them. No single step is to be overlooked or avoided. As you read them again, I trust that you will be able to recollect how each one played a significant role in one or another of the stories I have shared throughout the book.

The steps are as follows:

- *Clarity* with respect to your values and what matters most to you and your Great White Elephants, as they relate to ownership, power, and money.
- *Congruency* in your behaviors, actions and way of being with respect to your values and your Great White Elephants.
- *Connection* first with oneself and later with others about your values and Great White Elephants. To live with

clarity and congruency we must be connected to our authentic self. Another way to say this is *love* yourself.

- *Conversations* you must be willing to have with yourself and others regarding your values and Great White Elephants.
- *Commitment* to what you want to create for yourself and your family, based on your values and theirs which will keep the Great White Elephants away; commitment to continuing to deal with the Great White Elephants when they arise.

Have the clarity to know yourself—the good, the bad, and the ugly—and the Great White Elephants in all areas of your life. Get clear on your values, and live by them in a way that your actions are seen as being in alignment or congruent with those values. Connect your values to your actions as a new way of being. Connect yourself and your values, by becoming your values. Have continuous conversations with yourself if you find yourself slipping and not living or acting out of what you say your values are. Clean up situations where you have not been authentic. Develop new commitments that support and are in alignment with your values and way of being.

My wish and intention for you, as you reach the end of this book, is that you will find the courage to embark on a new journey, take the five steps outlined in this methodology so you can identify and ultimately release your own Great White Elephants and, in so doing, find your truth and fulfill your promise.

It has been both an honor and a privilege to serve as your guide and champion while you have spent time with the pages of this book. Thank you for this opportunity to inspire you.

As you have probably noted, I start most of my chapters with a quote, but I thought the one that follows was a fitting conclusion to this chapter, and book.

"It's a matter of switching gears, never looking back, and becoming the person today that you always dreamed you wanted to be. Entertain every thought, say every word, and make every decision from their point of view. Walk the way they would, dress the way they would dress, and spend your free time the way they would spend theirs. Choose the friends they would choose, eat the meals they would eat, and love and appreciate yourself the way they would.

These steps must come in order to facilitate change. There's no other option, no other way. But, since that person is who you really are, that makes this assignment downright effortless. Just stop being who you aren't!

— UNKNOWN —

Questions to Ponder...

1. What is your core Great White Elephant™?

2. What are you "othering" yourself for?

3. What are you pretending to ignore?

4. What is your Augustium?

5. What is your truth?

6. What is your promise?

Conclusion

If nothing ever changed, there'd be no butterflies.

— UNKNOWN —

I PROMISED YOU A BOOK ABOUT IMPROVING YOUR CHANCES of success in business succession planning and the transfer of wealth to the next generation, by having tools and a methodology to prepare yourself and the younger generation to achieve this outcome—with both intellectual and emotional integrity. You have also learned about the necessity of uncovering and facing your Great White Elephants (the missing conversations about unspoken issues and corrosive family dynamics), and the detrimental impact these creatures can have in your life and relationships if they remain under the table.

My hope is that you have become much more consciously aware of the capacity and capability you have in creating your own reality, your own world. Up to and at this particular point in your life, maybe you have created a lifestyle and way of being where everything is wonderful and fully aligned with what matters to you most, and is congruent with your values. Conversely, perhaps you haven't yet achieved this state of bliss. The question I present to you is this: Are the results of all your past efforts, and the current conditions of your life, really the results and conditions you always wanted and most earnestly desired, and are they truly representative of you and the values you strive to live out of and uphold? If your current living conditions are not representative of the results you really want to manifest in your life, when will it be the right time to make the changes you need to make to realize your dreams?

Ultimately, the design of your life is largely in your own hands. You do get to define how it looks and how it unfolds. The journey starts by acknowledging your Great White Elephants, understanding and releasing negative and potentially destructive beliefs and behaviors associated with the Great White Elephants of ownership, power, and money. With this understanding, each of us has the potential to create a sustainable and life-giving legacy that will survive intact for the benefit of future generations. Our values, beliefs, and behaviors about ownership, power, and money cannot be separated or compartmentalized from our valuables— our material wealth, investments, and assets.

You have come to this stage in your life. Something, perhaps something inside you, has led you to this book and the message it contains (or it might have been a gift, or recommended by a trusted source). Something about you has kept you believing that you deserve to be happy, experience joy, and perhaps deserve more than you currently have. You were born to do something special and unique, to live a life of value—for yourself and for others. In striving to always be the best you can be, and in working on eliminating the inauthentic versions of yourself, everything you have ever experienced in your life to this point has been to prepare and guide you to where you find yourself in this moment.

Now that you are really aware that your life, your destiny, your future and, ultimately, your family's future lie in your hands, imagine what you might do differently from this moment forward as a result of facing, being with, and embracing your Great White Elephants?

What will you do with the moments that are yours to create, now that you have revealed your Great White Elephants? No one else can take your place or create the life you want for yourself, or dance the dance you were born to dance. No one else can sing your song or write the story you were born to write. What will your story ultimately be?

Moving forward, who you become and what you do with and for your family starts right now. I believe that you have greatness in you and there is something uniquely glorious and magnificent about you, regardless of where you have been, and what you have done or not done with your life to this point. The moment you begin to think with integrity about yourself and how you feel about yourself, you will embrace the power within you that flows out of being congruent and authentic in the world. That energy will emerge and take over your life, it will feed you, guide you, encourage you, protect you, and sustain you; if you let it!

The power I am referring to here is the power to love unconditionally.

Learn to love yourself, the relationship you must nurture with yourself, love the life you create, love your family and embrace your greatness. You deserve it; it is your destiny.

Remember, nothing trumps love! Especially loving oneself!

SUGGESTED READINGS

Bachrach, W. (2000). *Values-based financial planning: The art of creating an inspiring financial strategy.* San Diego, CA: Aim High Publishing.

Blouin, B. (2003). *Labors of love: The legacy of inherited wealth, Book II.* Blacksburg, VA: Trio Press.

Blouin, B. & Gibson, K. (1997). *For love and/or money: The impact of inherited wealth on relationships.* Blacksburg, VA: Trio Press.

Brafman O. & Brafman R. (2008). *Sway: The irresistible pull of irrational behavior.* New York, NY: The Doubleday Publishing Group.

Chapman, G. (2010). *The five love languages: The secret to love that lasts.* Chicago, IL: Northfield Publishing.

Byrne, R. (2006). *The secret.* New York, NY: Atria Books & Hillsboro, OR: Beyond Words Publishing.

Chopra, D. (2003). *The spontaneous fulfillment of desire: Harnessing the infinite power of coincidence.* New York, NY: Harmony Books.

Cochell, P.L. & Zeeb, R.C. with Fowler, T. (2005). *Beating the Midas curse: Why does hard work and financial success lead to disaster for so many families, and how can you save yours?* West Lynn, OR: Heritage Institute Press.

Collins, J. (2001). *Good to great: Why some companies make the leap …
and others don't.* New York, NY: Collins.

Ferrucci, P. (2006). *The power of kindness: The unexpected benefits of
leading a compassionate life.* New York, NY: J.P. Tarcher/Penguin
Group.

Forward, S. & Buck, C. (1989). *Toxic parents: Overcoming their hurtful
legacy and reclaiming your life.* New York, NY: Bantam Books.

George, B. (2003). *Authentic leadership: Rediscovering the secrets to
creating lasting value.* San Francisco, CA: Jossey-Bass.

Gisel, T. (Dr. Seuss). (1990). *Oh, the places you'll go!* New York, NY:
Random House.

Grant, D. (2005). *The demon and the monk. My life of crime, addiction
and recovery.* Calgary, AB: IronWave Publishing.

Hendricks, G. (2003). *Conscious golf: The three secrets of success in
business, life and golf.* New York, NY: Rodale Inc.

Irvine, D. & Reger, J. (2006). *The authentic leader: It's about presence, not
position.* Sanford, FL: DC Press.

Johnson, S. (2003). *The present: The gift that makes you happier and more
successful at work and in life, today!* New York, NY: Doubleday.

Jones, L.B. (2004). *Jesus, life coach: Learn from the best.* Nashville, TN:
Thomas Nelson Inc.

Kouzes, J. & Posner, B.Z. (2006). *A leader's legacy.* San Francisco, CA:
Jossey-Bass.

Legge, P. with Holmes, D. (2001). *Who dares wins: An inspirational
collection of stories about those who succeeded by daring to live.*
Burnaby, BC: Eaglet Publishing.

Lencioni, P. (2002). *The five dysfunctions of a team: A leadership fable.* San Francisco, CA: Jossey-Bass.

O'Kelly, E. (2007). *Chasing daylight: How my forthcoming death transformed my life.* New York, NY: McGraw-Hill.

Peters, T. (1999). *The circle of innovation: You can't shrink your way to greatness.* New York, NY: Vintage.

Smedes, L.B. (1983). Forgiveness: The power to change the past. *Christianity Today* 27(1):22 – 26.

Trafford, A. (1982). *Crazy time: Surviving divorce and building a new life.* New York, NY: Harper Collins.

Vickers, M. (2002). *Becoming preferred: How to outsell your competition.* Calgary, AB: Summit Learning Systems Inc.

Williams, R. & Preisser, V. (2010). *Preparing heirs: Five steps to a successful transition of family wealth and values.* Brandon, OR: Robert Reed Publishers.

Williams, R. (1997). *For love and money: A comprehensive guide to the successful generational transfer of wealth.* Marina, CA: Monterey Institute.

Websites

Alberta Business Family Institute at the University of Alberta, School of Business, <www.business.ualberta.ca/abfi/>

BDO Dunwoody/COMPAS Report on Canadian Family-Owned Businesses (2003), <http://www.bdo.ca/library/publications/family business/succession/report.cfm>

Canadian Association of Family Enterprise, (CAFE),
<www.cafecanada.ca>

Dov Baron, <www.baronmastery.com> (Franco's personal mentor)

Family Firm Institute, <www.ffi.org>

Family Office Exchange, <www.foxexchange.com>

First Success Readiness Survey of Canadian Family-Owned Businesses
by Deloitte Centre for Tax Education and Research at the School of
Accounting and Finance, University of Waterloo (1999), <http://
accounting.uwaterloo.ca/tax.html>

Landmark Education, <www.landmarkeducation.com>

Loedstar, <www.loedstar.com>

Boaz Rauchwerger, Speaker, Trainer, Consultant & Author,
<www.boazpower.com>

Sauder School of Business at The University of British Columbia,
<www.sauder.ubc.ca>

Veritage Family Office, <www.veritage.ca> (Franco's company)

ABOUT THE BOOK

G*REAT WHITE ELEPHANT:*™ *WHY RICH KIDS HATE THEIR PARENTS* offers a simple methodology for improving your chances of achieving success in your business succession planning and wealth transition to the next generation, while leaving them properly prepared, both intellectually and emotionally, for that inheritance—ownership, power, and wealth, and all that this implies. This book offers a methodology for navigating the awkward conversations (the Great White Elephants) that can ultimately undermine a family and its desire to perpetuate the family's wealth.

Franco Lombardo draws from experience and shares candid stories wherein the strategies employed ensure values as well as valuables are successfully transitioned. Lombardo offers a model to better understand the interconnected role love plays in the bequeathing of wealth inter-generationally, and the impact ones Money Motto™ has on family relationships.

Lombardo compassionately challenges the current and universally applied approach to business succession planning and wealth transition and enables people to identify the ambivalent and often negative feelings, beliefs, and behaviors they hold towards ownership, power, and wealth. In *Great White Elephant:™ Why Rich Kids Hate Their Parents*, Lombardo gives you a roadmap to follow and the means to create a framework for success, ultimately bringing a family closer—all because they had the courage to face their Great White Elephants together.

About the Author

FRANCO LOMBARDO IS WELL KNOWN AND RESPECTED as a speaker, wealth advisor, and business coach who has been assisting some of North America's wealthiest families for the better part of twenty years. Through personal experience and his extensive work with family-owned business empires, Lombardo recognized and then identified a universal dynamic arising out of a largely ignored and previously unexamined connection between the individual and the relationship they have with money and wealth. His work both examines and illuminates the impact this unexplored relationship with money and wealth can have for clients with respect to the other relationships they have with their family, business activities, community, philanthropic goals, and their plans for wealth transition and business succession planning.

Combining more than a decade of training in the facilitation of personal growth with his vast experience as a wealth advisor, Lombardo developed an investigative process that invites each member of a family group with whom he is working to recognize and then integrate the relationship they have with money and

wealth, firstly for themselves, and then align that relationship with every other aspect of their lives, other family members, business activities, community, philanthropic goals and their plans for wealth transition and business succession planning. His process is called *Life After Wealth*,® and was described in his first book of the same title: *Life after Wealth:*® *When is Enough Enough?* (2003). Further development of his approach to wealth transition and business succession planning came in his second book: *Money Motto:*™ *The Path to Authentic Wealth*™*!* (2007). *The Great White Elephant:*™ *Why Rich Kids Hate Their Parents* (2012), is the culmination of all that he has learned in the past decade with respect to successfully facilitating wealth transition and business succession planning for family-owned businesses.

Franco is also a highly sought-after speaker around the English-speaking world and has spoken to *The Canadian Institute of Chartered Accountants* (CICA), *The Society of Trust and Estate Practitioners* (STEP), *The Family Office Association, Young Presidents' Organization* (YPO), and *Tiger21*. He has appeared as a guest on national television programs including *Money Talks* on BNN and *The Morning Show* on Global Television.

Passionate and engaging, Franco is considered a leading expert on the psychology of money, its dynamic influence within families, and the profound impact it has upon a family's legacy which is contingent upon their ability to successfully negotiate the process of wealth transition. He is committed to assisting individuals and families uncover their Money Motto,™ facilitating a greater awareness in his clients concerning the relationship they have with money and wealth so that they will be far more assured that the wealth they have to bequeath will empower their children (successors) to find, claim, and embrace their own highest potential.

FOR MORE INFORMATION

To contact the author, please visit

www.moneymotto.com

or e-mail:

francol@veritage.ca

Read about Franco Lombardo's first book

LIFE *after* WEALTH®
When is Enough Enough?

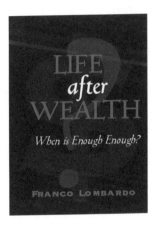

*L*ife *after Wealth*® offers a blueprint for creating an authentic relationship with money, based on your life purpose and life values. Lively stories and thought-provoking questions provide valuable tools to help you discover your definition of true wealth. This book helps you release your old ideas about money and guides you to embrace a deeper understanding of who you are, why you are here, and how you go about creating true wealth through the choices you make every day.

Contents

- Dedication ix
- Acknowledgments xi
- Preface xv
- Foreword by Dana Green xvii

• • •

- Introduction.. 1
1 The Retirement Myth.. 9
2 The Ego & Money.. 17
3 The Values Conversation....................................... 25
4 Life Purpose... 39
5 Life Values... 49
6 Aligning Values, Money & Time............................ 67
7 Love & Money 77
8 Kids & Money 89
9 Life Giving 107
- Conclusion 117

• • •

- Suggested Readings... 121
- About the Author... 123
- Philosophy & Contribution.................................... 125
- How to Contact Us 127

What people said about *Life after Wealth*®

"For those desiring REAL wealth in their life, this book offers us life-changing wisdom and practical suggestions. Franco's human perspective on financial planning will enrich your life. This thought-provoking book goes from realizing financial freedom to living a legacy of significance and meaning."

DAVID IRVINE, author of
Simple Living in a Complex World

"*Life after Wealth* is the kind of book you read in one sitting and then ponder for days, weeks and months. If you are looking for a way to take your life to a more meaningful level, where each day is filled with deep abundance you have found your road map.

Franco Lombardo has created a road map to financial and spiritual abundance. *Life after Wealth* is so good that I read it in one sitting. If you are looking to lead a life on-purpose, where your dreams come true and your financial worries disappear…then you must read this book!"

DAVID BACH, national best-selling author of
Smart Women Finish Rich and *Smart Couples Finish Rich*

"If you're ready to spend your time and money doing what matters most to you, this book is a must-read. Thank you Franco for reminding us that our money is for living."

JANET AMARE, author of *Soul Purpose*

"Finally, a book that speaks about the value of money. Franco Lombardo opens hearts and minds in this wonderful work."

LAURIE BETH JONES, author of
Jesus, CEO; The Path, and *Jesus, Inc.*

"This book provides you with meaningful insight about combining your purpose in life with your financial goals and enjoying the fruits of your labour. This is a unique perspective from the financial services industry. Enjoy and think."

RICHARD STONE
President & CEO *Stone Funds*

"*Life after Wealth* is a guide to living with a wise and wonderful message around the meaning of money. This book will remind you of what is really important and how to achieve it."

ROSS BUCHANAN
President, *Strategic Results International* and author of
License to Lead and *Life without Limits!*

"Franco's book, *Life after Wealth,* is not about answers, it is about asking the right questions. Franco's process brilliantly identifies your key financial drivers, helps you understand your personal blueprint for money and shows you how to move from financial security to "Self-security." Read it. Apply it. Enjoy the abundance!"

MICHAEL VICKERS, author of
Becoming Preferred

Read about Franco Lombardo's second book

MONEY MOTTO™
The Path to Authentic Wealth™!

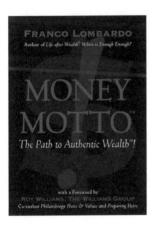

*M*oney Motto™ *The Path to Authentic Wealth*™! offers readers a blueprint for examining their relationship with money and wealth from their own frame of reference. The process starts with recollections you've had since childhood—both in general terms and as they specifically relate to money.

Drawing upon his own experience, Franco Lombardo shares candid stories—both personal and professional—from his work within the wealth advising industry, asks thought-provoking questions, and outlines a step-by-step process for discovering and understanding your Money Motto™. In opening the door on a long-overlooked aspect of wealth management, Franco Lombardo offers a process for readers to better understand the values they hold about money and wealth.

In *Money Motto:* ^{TM} *The Path to Authentic Wealth* ^{TM}*!* Lombardo compassionately challenges and enables people to identify and then release negative and ineffective behaviors and beliefs they may hold towards money, and create a more authentic relationship with wealth that will support the realization of their goals and dreams.

CONTENTS

- Dedication xi
- Acknowledgments xiii
- Foreword by Roy Williams xix
- Preface xxi

• • •

1 The Pursuit of "More"..1
2 Image Management 11
3 Life Goes Where You Focus....................................29
4 Bridging the Gap:
    Components of Wealth Management 47
5 The Money Motto:^{TM}
    Who Is Really Running Your Life?..................67
6 A Path to Authentic Wealth^{TM} 83
- Conclusion 101

• • •

- Suggested Readings 105
- About the Book 109
- About the Author...111
- For More Information 113

Early Praise for *Money Motto*™

"I continue to be amazed at the energy, passion, and transparency that Franco brings to the way we manage our money, and how this is reflected in the vulnerability he brought to the writing of this book. After you have read *Money Motto*™ you should be well on your way to permanently changing the way you use your wealth. In an age where more, more, more is too often our mantra, it is refreshing to shed a different light on the subject. The key to authentic wealth is to find your authentic self! Through this book, Franco is more than capable of being your guide."

LAWRENCE BARNES, CEO,
Canadian Association of Family Enterprise (CAFÉ)

"This is the future. If you have money and want to ensure you stay in the driver's seat to reach personal fulfillment and build a better world, this is a must-read. Thanks Franco!"

VICKI BRILZ, entrepreneur who sold her successful business.

"When it comes to creating a great relationship with money, Franco Lombardo knows what he's talking about! He is living proof that there is a process for creating such a relationship. This book is the roadmap both to creating a positive self-image and financial prosperity."

BOAZ RAUCHWERGER, speaker, trainer, coach,
and author of *The Tiberias Transformation*.

"At last—the true definition of wealth is discovered and explored!"

LAURA NORTH, certified coach.

"Franco's book is about money, but it's not really about money. It's about your *life* and how, by examining your deep-seated beliefs and values about wealth, money can become a tool for living authentically. This book is a wonderful guide for your journey towards understanding and creating authentic wealth in your life."

DAVID IRVINE, co-author of *The Authentic Leader*
and author of *Becoming Real*.

"*Money Motto*™ can change your relationship with money. It's a great tool!"

MARCI SHIMOFF, co-author, *Chicken Soup for the Woman's Soul*
and featured teacher in the hit film, *The Secret*.

"This book is a valuable map to understanding your true relationship with money—an imperative for anyone who wishes to live a life of deeper meaning, significance, and purpose."

JIM REGER, co-author of *The Authentic Leader*.

"This is Franco Lombardo's second unique book that examines wealth. It is insightful and packed with great wisdom. Learn from Franco. I do."

PETER LEGGE, LLD (Hon), businessman, speaker
and author of *Who Dares Wins* and *Make Your Life a Masterpiece*.

"Finally a book that speaks about the value of money. Franco Lombardo opens hearts and minds in this wonderful work."

LAURIE BETH JONES, author of *Jesus, CEO; The Path,
Jesus, Inc.*, and *Jesus, Life Coach*.

"A frank, refreshing, and often poignant look at an important and timeless topic, ultimately forcing each of us to confront the meaning we want from our lives and the nature of the legacy we want to leave behind."

> BARRY Z. POSNER, PhD, Dean & Professor of Leadership,
> Santa Clara University, and co-author of *The Leadership Challenge*,
> *Encouraging the Heart*, and *A Leader's Legacy*

"Mr. Lombardo has crafted an insightful description of how we behave through the use of our money. This is far more than a discussion of wealth! It provides a prescription and points us in the direction of a path which will lead towards a successful life."

> BILL BONE, President of a Canadian Business Family Office

"Lombardo's work is a helpful and unembellished look at those for whom money is an emotional crutch. Family business founders and successors should heed his essential lesson: Money is easy, life and family are hard, but far more fulfilling."

> JOSEPH H. ASTRACHAN, PhD, Director, Cox Family Enterprise Center
> & Wachovia Eminent Scholar & Chair of Family Business
> Coles College of Business, Kennesaw State University.

"Franco's done it again! If you read his first book, *Life after Wealth*,® then you understand the impact that his strategies can have on your personal wealth and overall attitude towards money. His new book asks some excellent questions that will help you uncover your personal Money Motto.™ CEOs who want to improve the financial mindset of their corporation would be well advised to follow Franco's strategies and develop their corporate Money Motto.™"

> MICHAEL VICKERS, best-selling author of *Becoming Preferred*.